BECOMING
PEOPLE
of the Way

REV. DR. ROBERT HOFFMAN

ISBN 978-1-64515-283-5 (paperback)
ISBN 978-1-64515-284-2 (digital)

Christian Faith Publishing, Inc.
832 Park Avenue
Meadville, PA 16335
www.christianfaithpublishing.com

Printed in the United States of America

Becoming: God is never done with us. We are, hopefully, always becoming.

People: This journey is too hard for us to go it alone. We need to live within a community that will support and challenge us.

of The Way: We believe God calls us to a new way of living.

*Saul went to the Chief Priest and got arrest warrants to take
to the meeting places in Damascus, so that if he found any
one there belonging to the Way, whether men or women,
he could arrest them and bring them to Jerusalem.*

—Acts 9:1–2

CONTENTS

INTRODUCTION

In 1956, TA Kantonen wrote, "What is this thing you call stewardship? If it represents only clever means which practical-minded Americans have devised for raising money, interest in it soon subsides. But if it can be shown to be vital Christian faith in action, then it raises the hope that there may be the beginning of a new awakening and renewal, a new coming of the Spirit."[1]

Those are powerful words. Over the next sixty-plus years, did any of the various Christian denominations in the United States experience a "new awakening and renewal" through a deeper appreciation of stewardship? I am not aware of any. So why another book on stewardship?

During that same period, dozens of books were published that dealt with this topic, including such titles as *The Steward, Giving to God, Behind the Stained Glass Window, The Paradox of Generosity, God and Mammon in America, Making the Annual Pledge Drive Obsolete, Virtue and Affluence,* and *To Give and Give Again.* These are fine books that I found to be worthwhile reading. Have any of them had a demonstrable effect on giving within the church? Not to my knowledge.

In fact, over the last few years, I have had several conversations with denominational leaders, regional leaders, and conference leaders as well as parish pastors who are ready to give up the word *stewardship* altogether. The claim is that the word is so misunderstood and carries so much unhappy baggage, it is no longer salvageable. The preference seems to be to use such words as *generosity* and *gratitude.* I, for one, am not ready to give up.

In 1920, G. K. Chesterton wrote, "Christianity has not been tried and found wanting. It has been found difficult and rarely tried."[2] I am convinced that the same can be said for stewardship.

In 1993, the Rev. Dr. Herbert W. Chilstrom, then serving as the presiding bishop of the Evangelical Lutheran Church in America (ELCA), made a presentation to a national gathering in which he said, "Over the past twenty years we have cut down forest after forest of trees, to get the lumber, to create the pulp, to make the paper on which we have been printing our stewardship materials. And still, it seems, that our giving is going down. Why?"

I happened to be sitting in the audience when Dr. Chilstrom made this observation. At the time I was serving as a stewardship specialist on the staff of the ELCA. I was one of twenty-eight field staff that served in various geographical regions across the United States. I found it to be an exceptional group of people.

At that time, our national team gathered in Chicago at least twice a year to (1) learn about new materials that would soon be made available to the congregations we served; (2) share information about new programs we had developed in our own regions; and (3) have an opportunity to meet with people who were thought to be doing excellent work in the area of stewardship.

What Bishop Chilstrom apparently did not know was that about a year before he made his observation, our team had met with John and Sylvia Ronsvalle, the president and executive vice-president of *empty tomb, inc.* Their organization was then, and continues to be, among other things, a research organization that gathers data on giving from among a wide range of denominations. In preparation for our meeting with the Ronsvalles, our staff was sent a booklet entitled, *North American Conference On Christian Philanthropy 1990.*[3] The booklet included an article that the Ronsvalles had written entitled "Giving Trends and Their Implications for the 1990s."

The first two pages of "Giving Trends" provide some very interesting information on what is happening economically to the typical American household. Their key observation was that while the total amount of offerings given to churches was increasing, it represented a decreasing percentage of the income of those households.

The Ronsvalles' sense was that church leaders were not aware of this negative trend.

In preparation for a pilot project designed to reverse the negative trends found in their 1988 stewardship study, the authors interviewed sixty congregations from ten denominations as well as a variety of denominational officials. Here are some of their observations:

- Money is a difficult topic for the church to discuss.
- Pastors feel ill-prepared for stewardship tasks.
- There is a "pay-the-bills" mentality within the church.
- Congregation members have become consumers purchasing services (youth programs, nice buildings) rather than stewards returning a portion of what they've been given by God.
- The general feeling was that attitudes toward money and stewardship require deep changes but that those changes will not come about easily or quickly.

As I read through these observations, all sorts of bells and whistles were going off in my head. What they described was precisely what I had been observing in my work with congregations for the previous five years. However, what really caught my attention was when they introduced the term *dysfunctional patterns*. They suggested that one might term *dysfunctional* as "the inability to act on one's desires in appropriate ways because of established patterns of counterproductive behavior."[4]

The authors went on to suggest that at this stage, more information was not going to be the solution. It was going to require approaches that identified and addressed the established counterproductive behavior.

About two weeks later, I traveled to Chicago to our team meeting. I was anxious to meet the Ronsvalles and hear more about what they were observing. During our second morning in Chicago, John and Sylvia made a very informative presentation to our entire team. We took a brief break after their opening presentation. When we regathered, our team was informed we had a few minutes to discuss or ask questions about the morning presentation. It was then time for lunch. As our group sat down for lunch, I sensed great energy in the room. There were numerous lively conversations going on. I, for one, was very much looking forward to a discussion of the material in the article we were assigned to read. I was very interested to hear what the director of our unit thought were some of the "deep changes" that *we* would need to make. When we returned from lunch, we were informed that there would be no discussion of their article.

I was stunned. Why not discuss the article? Was it too challenging to hear *we* might be part of the problem? I was then, and still am, convinced that the Ronsvalles' observations and suggestions were just what the church needs to hear. It has been my experience that there continues to be very few willing to listen.

Upon returning home from our team meeting, I contacted the Ronsvalles and thanked them for their helpful work. I subsequently put together a two-page summary[4] of their observations. I have used it with denominational leaders, bishops, deans, conference leaders, and with well over 400 congregations.

Since most of the people I have worked with have indicated they were unclear as to what *dysfunctional* meant, I devised a brief illustration. I asked the group I was with to imagine that we had a standard household vacuum in front of us. I stipulated it was plugged in. I then offered four examples:

- Example 1: If I press the On/Off button and the motor comes on and the machine is able to pick up the typical dust and dirt on the floor, we would say that the machine is functional.

- Example 2: If I press the button and the motor comes on but it is capable of picking up only very light dust but not any heavier dirt, we would say the machine is malfunctional.

- Example 3: If I press the button and the motor does not come on, we would call the machine nonfunctional.

- Example 4: If I press the button and the motor comes and it begins to spew dirt all over the floor, we would say the machine is dysfunctional. It is having the opposite effect of what we intended. It is counterproductive to the original intention of the machine.

This little illustration usually got people laughing a little. After the laughter died down, I would typically ask the group, "So where do you think you will begin making your changes?" At the point, the room always became silent.

In summary, I can report the following: (1) Not one group with whom I shared the Ronsvalles' essay ever challenged the authors' conclusions; (2) None of these groups were ready to identify any changes they needed to make.

It has been said that the definition of *insanity* is "doing the same thing over and over and expecting different results." I keep meeting with church leaders who continue to refuse to change anything they are doing in stewardship but expect their results to improve.

Near the end of "Giving Trends,"[5] the Ronsvalles suggest that the solution to our dysfunctional habits will require something beyond more information. We will need to be able to (1) identify our counterproductive behavior and (2) offer a process for implementing the changes that will be required. That is the purpose of this book.

In February, 1973, I began the interview process for the position of assistant pastor of St. Paul's Lutheran Church in Mt. Holly, New Jersey. I do not recall what questions the search committee asked me. I do recall a question that I asked them. "What does this congregation do well?"

One of members of the committee said, "Stewardship."

The first thought that came to mind was that at no time during the three years that I spent in seminary, did I ever hear anyone even use the word *stewardship*. If the word was not even mentioned in seminary, how important could it be?

Why another book on stewardship? 1.) Because I think the Ronsvalles were absolutely right in their observations. All of the congregations I've worked with have had a number of stewardship practices that were, and are, counterproductive. In most cases they had been "doing it this way for so long" that no one ever thought it was unhelpful, let alone in need of change. 2.) Most congregations really don't understand the word *stewardship* and its profound implications. 3.) Because of these first two, we have very little idea of what a congregation that is "good at stewardship" would even look like or how it got that way.

Why another book on stewardship? Because I was eventually called to serve that congregation in Mt. Holly. Those next five years had a profound impact on the rest of my life and ministry. I was able to witness, up close and personal, what stewardship ministry is all about. I am convinced we do not want to give up the word *stewardship*. My hope is that by sharing some things I have experienced, you will come to find this ministry as exciting as I do.

CHAPTER ONE

The Adventure Begins

*The real voyage of discovery consists not in seeking
new landscapes, but in having new eyes.*

—Marcel Proust

I began my ministry at St. Paul's on July 1, 1973. My introduction to stewardship at St. Paul's came six weeks later. The congregation's stewardship committee had planned an every-member visit. The plan called for the two pastors to each visit six members of the twelve-member church council. When I first heard this, I went running to the senior pastor to confess that I had no idea of what I was supposed to do. He assured me that it would not be too difficult. All the members of the council were used to completing a pledge card. Many of them were already tithing. It would just be an opportunity to share some stories.

Since we were already on the topic of stewardship, Dave, the senior pastor, decided to take this opportunity to have some further conversation. He asked me if I was familiar with the term *giving records*. I said no. He went on to explain that each congregation keeps a record of the offerings given by each household. If a pledge has been made, this is also recorded.

Dave made it quite clear that he thought it was very important for a pastor to have access to a congregation's giving information. He did at St. Paul's. As one of the pastors, I had access to that information as well. He was well aware that some congregations did not want their pastor to have access to this information. He also explained that he knew of pastors who did not want to look at this information. He strongly encouraged me to know this information.[1]

Dave continued, "We say that our giving records are kept confidential, and they are. Having said that, you would be wise to assume that people will know what you are giving.

"If you write a check, it goes to the counters. They see your gifts. If you are going to encourage generous giving, you had better be giving generously."

That too was very sage advice.

A few months later, I had another conversation with Dave. This one was about church finances. He indicated that he thought pastors needed to have a basic understanding of church finance. You didn't have to be a CPA, but you do need to let your lay leaders know you know.

Dave went on to say that he knew of more than one pastor who said they did not attend finance committee meetings because they did not understand "that stuff." If a pastor announces to their congregation that they do not understand finances, they basically disqualify themselves as a stewardship leader. Why would a lay person listen to someone talk about the importance of giving after that person had already announced that they didn't really understand financial matters?

It turned out the visitation happened exactly as predicted. I was readily welcomed into six homes. I was very uneasy prior to the first visit. I was not sure what I was going to say or how I was going to subtly lead the conversation to the topic of stewardship. It so happened my first visit was with a person who had been a member of the call committee. Our opening conversation was about the call process and how I thought it went. After about ten minutes, my host said something like, "Pastor, I know you are here to do a stewardship visit. Why don't we start by me sharing with you a little bit about how I became a steward?"

I had a very similar experience during each of my next five visits. As I listened to each of these lay leaders, I began to get a sense of what had happened at St. Paul's.

About eight years before, the congregation had called a new pastor. He quickly picked up the nickname PC (Pastor Christiansen). PC had a passion for stewardship, most specifically, the importance of generous giving in the life of a Christian.

One of the first things PC did upon his arrival was to set up a series of in-home visits with the leaders of the congregation. He got to know them, and they got to know him. He shared with them his understanding of the importance of giving in the life of a Christian. He talked about this being a key priority in his ministry. He expressed his hope that they would be excited by what he had in mind. All of this, he was quick to clarify, is possible because, first of all, we understand ourselves as truly blessed.

Since it was important for an individual Christian to be a generous giver, PC explained that it only made sense that the congregation model this. Since PC spoke of the importance of intentionally sharing a percentage of one's income, it only made sense that the congregation do the same. Given that we are all invited to offer our first fruits to the Lord (see Deut. 26:1–2), it only made sense that the congregation do the same. The congregation would later vote to do their sharing in terms of a percentage of income *and* make it a first-fruits gift.

PC's constant theme was "God is able to provide you with every blessing in abundance so that by always having enough of everything, you may share abundantly in every good work" (2 Corinthians 9:8).

Looking back now, it seems pretty clear that PC knew what he was doing. Most of the literature on organizational transformation had not been written in 1965, but that is what PC did. He knew he needed to change the culture of the congregation. To accomplish that he knew one step was to help the congregation begin thinking and acting in terms of abundance, not scarcity.

One of the ways he did this was to consistently teach and preach on the theme of how blessed we all are by God. But there was also a second piece. PC became the pastor of a congregation that had, for many years, been told that the reason we give our offerings is to "support the church we love." Indeed, many of the people were already very faithful supporters of the church. PC, however, wanted to move them from being loyal supporters to becoming faithful stewards. He stated this quite clearly over and over again.

Why haven't all of our years of stewardship work across the denominations been more effective?

I think one reason is because we never took seriously the importance of the culture of a congregation. Not too surprisingly, most of our congregations reflect the culture that surrounds them. Obviously, the culture that surrounds them in our United States is one that assumes scarcity.[2] My observation has been that no person (or organization) will shift from a scarcity mentality to an abundance mentality by simply reading an article or a book. You have to act it out and experience that this is true.

PC was also very intentional about getting to know his leaders. He was always on the lookout for people who could talk about their giving. Over time, he pulled together a strong stewardship committee that included some key leaders from within the congregation. There was never a chairperson of the St. Paul's stewardship committee who got that job because "no one else would do it." PC made sure a mature steward held that position of leadership. As Wallace Fisher wrote, "The bland can lead the bland, but only to be more bland."[3]

When I've shared this story with people over the years, the consistent response has been, "PC introduced some kind of legalism."

My response is always, "Not at all." At no time was pledging or tithing ever made a requirement within the congregation. I never heard anyone quoting some portion of the Old or New Testament as a proof text that demanded compliance. On the other hand, from the stories I heard, PC did talk openly about what he expected of his leaders. Example, it was common knowledge that all persons elected to the congregation council would be "expected" to pledge.

This open talk about money and giving was not reserved for just the members of the council. All persons who expressed interest in joining the congregation were invited to an evening meeting. Ostensibly, the purpose of the gathering was for the perspective new members to meet the members of the church council. In fact, it was at this meeting that several leaders gave personal testimony as to the importance of giving in their lives, including their decision to tithe. Those who were joining the congregation were invited to begin the spiritual discipline of filling out a pledge card. There was no mention of a budget that needed funding. They were also encouraged, if they were not doing so already, to consider making their commitment to giving in terms of a percent of their annual income. Were these requirements? No.

During this first round of visits, I also heard stories to the effect that not everyone was pleased with PC. Over time, some people began suggesting he should spend more time tending to their needs and less time talking about making disciples. Being invited to a make a deeper commitment can scare some people (see Luke 18:18–23). Indeed, several families actually left the congregation over this issue. This too was an important thing for me to learn.

After five years, PC decided he wanted to move on. What I found very significant as I listened to this story was the response of the congregation's leadership. As it considered the qualities they wanted in their next pastor, they did *not* say, "We've been focusing on stewardship long enough. Let's go in another direction."

Rather, they understood the importance of this emphasis and intentionally sought a pastor who also had a keen interest in stewardship. They found one.

Pastor Dave arrived and picked up where PC left off. He too loved to talk about the importance of giving in the life of a Christian. He took PC's mantra "we are blessed" and expanded it to "Blessed to be a blessing" (Genesis 12:2). Under Dave's leadership the congregation continued to increase the percentage of offering income they gave away. The continued message was that "we give because we are blessed and are called by God to be a blessing to others." There was no mention of funding anything.

About three years into Dave's ministry, it was becoming increasingly apparent that the workload was too much for one person. A decision was made to hire an assistant pastor. However, the leadership made it clear to the congregation that the funds that would be needed to support this second pastor were *not* going to come from simply cutting back on what the congregation was giving away. The commitment to be "a blessing to others" would remain.

This is the situation I walked into on July 1, 1973. St. Paul's was a pretty healthy congregation. I didn't realize how healthy it was until I started talking with friends from seminary. We were all just starting in our first calls. Most of my friends were called to congregations that were just getting by financially. There was pressure to cut back, rather than expand, the sharing their congregations were able to do. Their leaders always seemed to be afraid there was not enough.

Just like any other congregation, St. Paul's experienced an uneven cash flow. Finances usually got tight in the late summer. Yet even as this was happening, few of the leaders got too worried. There was little or no anxious reactivity[4] around money issues.

Again, I was not aware of what I was learning as I was in the midst of it. Looking back now, I realize I was observing what it was like to be what Edwin H. Friedman[5] would later call a non-anxious presence when it came to money. I observed this behavior for five years. Over time, this way of leading apparently, unconsciously, sunk in.

In my five years at St. Paul's, I discovered how much fun stewardship ministry could be. I enjoyed the opportunity to talk openly with people about their giving. I was inspired watching people mature in their faith. It was exciting to be a part of a community of people that lived with "glad and generous hearts" (Acts 2:46).

The congregation continued to expand its sharing, including its financial support of some local community projects. Often, people from our congregation became active in those projects and programs. St. Paul's developed a reputation within the Mt. Holly area of being a congregation that cared.

Again, it was only later that I would come to more fully understand the critical significance of a congregation's reputation. Our congregation continued to grow in worship attendance, offering income, and new members. All of which seemed to confirm what I had learned in my study of biology. You don't have to force healthy organisms to grow—they do so naturally.

During my time at St. Paul's, I obviously became infected by the stewardship virus. Even as I was having all of this fun, there was a part of me that started asking, "Wouldn't be great if more congregations could experience this? As we used to ask in biology lab, "Can this experiment be reproduced?" Is it possible to transfer this kind of excitement to another congregation? Or was what happened at St. Paul's a one-time experience?

Why another book on stewardship? Because I have been on this journey for a long time. I continue to encounter pastors and congregations that keep doing the same old stuff and expecting different results. The Ronsvalles were right. Much of what we are doing in stewardship is not only not working, but it is also counterproductive. Twenty-five years ago, the Ronsvalles told us, "We need to make some deep changes, but those changes will not come about easily or quickly." I think it is time we listen.

Why another book on stewardship? I experienced a more excellent way.

CHAPTER TWO

It Is Repeatable

If you live your religion, you will become different.

—Dom Helder Camara

Even as I made the decision to leave Mt. Holly, I knew the experience there had changed my understanding of parish ministry. I knew that I wanted to see if what I had experienced there could be replicated in another congregation. I had a general idea in mind, but I was also aware that every congregation is quite different. Whatever congregation I'd eventually be called to serve, I assumed it would be several months before any significant decisions would have to be made.

On Sunday morning, October 9, 1977, I was called to be the pastor of the Lutheran Church of the Apostles in Turnersville, New Jersey. I told the leadership that morning that I would accept the call. The words were barely out of my mouth when the council vice-president mentioned that there was a council meeting to take place two days later. He asked me to attend. I said I would.

At that Tuesday night meeting, I was informed of a few issues that had not come up during the interview process: (1) there was a leak in the roof over the worship space, and when it rained, the water would fall on the organ; (2) the congregation had a $25,000 balloon payment on a mortgage due in six months, and no money had been set aside; (3) the parking lot, which I had observed was unpaved, became a field of mud when it rained; (4) the council had voted to stop sending money to our denomination eighteen months ago because of the financial crisis they were currently experiencing. At my first meeting with this group of leaders, before I'd even officially started, they wanted to know which of these I was going to take care of first.

I reminded them that I was not due to start for almost a month. I told them I would do some thinking and that we could discuss these issues in November. They agreed.

I knew, going in, that this congregation was experiencing some difficulty. I also knew from my experience at Mt. Holly that this congregation was not going to get healthy overnight. I had no magic formula. It would be a process that would require several years. It never occurred to me that some very important decisions would need to be made so soon after arriving. I also sensed that how I proceeded with the four issues the council gave me that first night would be very important in terms of setting a tone for the years ahead. When our council gathered for its November meeting, I knew my leaders were anxious to hear my answer. I told them the issue I wanted to address first was number 4, our sharing with our denomination. The current treasurer was heard to say, "You're nuts!"

It was pretty clear that the current leadership thought they were in the midst of a financial crisis. They were operating in a scarcity mode; they were convinced there was not enough. I hadn't planned on addressing this issue so soon, but here it was. I suggested that in preparing the budget for 1978, we set a percentage figure of our total offering income and pledge to give that percentage away as a first-fruits gift.

It was at that point that I was warned by my leaders that if the congregation did agree to this, it was possible that I might not get paid, at least not on time. I said I would be willing to live with that possibility as long as I was paid before all the other bills. It was my sense that since I was the one foolish enough to agree, they would go along.

As we talked further, I was able to explain that I didn't just look at number 4. I'd also looked at the first three and had some suggestions as to how to move forward in each case. In fact, one of my suggestions was so simple, I was surprised no one had thought it. I was not going to live in the house the congregation owned. They could sell this house and come up with the funds to pay off the $25,000 balloon payment.

I learned later as I became more familiar with family systems theory, that one of the problems with anxiety is that it tends to limit people's ability to come up with creative options. The term Peter Steinke uses is *imaginative gridlock*.[5]

Obviously, one of the things I had learned from PC was the importance of giving. He also spoke of the importance of modeling. How can a congregation invite its people to be generous in their sharing if the congregation shares little or nothing? Then, too, I knew that if I waited to address our sharing beyond ourselves until my entire council thought we could afford it, it would never happen.

It was not until years later that I realized how common a practice it was for congregations, when money gets tight, to cut their budget. Of course, the first place that gets cut in the budget is their sharing. I understand the logic. It so happens that it does not work. In fact, it is not only not helpful, but it is also counterproductive. The Ronsvalles were on to something! And yet to this day, I see congregation after congregation still doing this very thing. How can a congregation tell its people to trust that God will provide and then refuse to do so as an organization?

Other than having to make a couple of decisions almost immediately upon arriving, I never forgot that helping the congregation become healthier was going to take time. It was going to be a process. Remembering how PC started, I began making in-home visits to the members of our council and other leaders. I needed to get to know them and let them get to know me. Then, too, I had learned to be on the lookout for stewards. And yes, I found some.

After about four months, I began recruiting a stewardship team. Having completed my first round of visits and having had some helpful conversations, I had a pretty good sense of who would be good people to recruit. I had access to the giving records of the congregation and looked at that information as well. In a couple of instances, there were people I had in mind for the stewardship team that were already involved on other committees within the congregation. I met with them and asked them if they'd be willing to accept a new committee assignment. Two agreed. One did not. That was just fine

When our new stewardship team met for the first time, I suggested that we had four responsibilities we needed to keep in mind.

1. We need to grow in our own understanding of stewardship. We need to keep learning.
2. We need to provide opportunities for our members to grow in their understanding and practice of stewardship.
3. We need to provide oversight to policies and procedures to make sure the congregation was acting like a good steward.
4. We need to provide leadership for the annual response program.

For the first several months, our stewardship team spent a lot of time on relationship building. At the time, I subscribed to a monthly magazine called *The Clergy Journal*.[2] Each edition had an article on stewardship. We began reading and discussing that article each time we met.

The questions we kept in mind were the following: What new insight did we gain? Was there a way to use it? Was there anything worth sharing with our congregation?

These discussions eventually opened the door to various people sharing their stewardship stories, typically who taught them to be stewards. News of these conversations began to percolate through the rest of the congregation. Other members of the congregation could not imagine how people seemed to actually enjoy attending a stewardship meeting.

After about a year, our Stewardship Team leader, as she gave her monthly report to the council, would share what we had been talking about at our last meeting. She would then invite the other council members into the conversation.

About the same time, a member of the Stewardship Team came to me and said it was a shame more people could not experience what our team was experiencing. We talked for a while and decided it was time to begin a Wednesday-evening Bible study. This study became a great setting to have people share their faith and for me to learn who was growing in their faith.

In the meantime, if the topic of money or possessions were ever in one of our assigned readings on a Sunday, I preached on them. However, it never became an occasion for me to beg or plead for increased offerings. We were not going to act or talk scarcity.

We finished 1978 with all of our bills paid and had kept our commitment to share 8 percent off the top. Most of my leaders were convinced that this was a fluke and would never happen again. We continued the commitment for 1979, and we made it again. I will never forget the meeting we had to propose a budget for 1980. Our council president, a man of few words, said that he never thought that sharing off the top would work. He continued, "I can come up with no logical reason as to how this has happened other than the hand of God. I do not want to lose the momentum we have. I hereby propose that we increase our sharing figure to 10 percent for 1980."

There seems to be the perception that people believe their way into acting, i.e., if you get people to believe something strongly enough, they will act on that belief. I have observed that the opposite is true. If you can get people to act a certain way, they will actually start believing. Apostles did not start sharing 8 percent off the top because of great faith. They agreed to it, but most assumed that it would never work. They knew we would come up short. After two years of making it, they were now ready to step out in faith.

About three years after I arrived, the church treasurer had to resign because of a job change. As much as I liked and respected the man, he tended to be one of those people for whom the glass was always half empty. We were able to replace him with a woman who not only had a good sense of stewardship but was also known to be a very competent accountant. From then on, when it was time for her report at the monthly council meeting, instead of droning on with thirty minutes of bad news, she would typically say, "We're good. Any questions?" There were rarely any. If Dorothy said we were good, we were good.

Over the next few years, I could sense the congregation culture was slowly but noticeably changing. It was in my fifth year that we experienced a real breakthrough.

One of the events that had been going on long before I arrived was the annual Tag Sale. It happened every fall. People would rent a table from the congregation. The rental money was used to help fund the annual budget. People could rent one or more tables. They would use the tables to display items they wanted to sell to the public. The renters, of course, would keep the proceeds from their sales.

For several years, I argued that having a tag sale was not a good idea. The fact that our congregation needed to do a fundraiser was sending the wrong message to the surrounding community. My recommendation that we stop having tag sales was consistently voted down. After four years, at least we shifted the proceeds from the table rentals from our annual budget to a youth-ministry fund. Even then, because of our great location (on a major highway) and the great fun people had on the Saturday of the sale, very few were ready to give up the Tag Sale.

It was a Saturday in the fall of 1982. Our Tag Sale was open for business. People were stopping to look at the items on our tables. Our people were interacting with the public. It so happened that our council vice president got into a conversation with one of our shoppers. The shopper acknowledged that she had been at several of our tag sales in the past. She and her husband liked to stop by and "support a small struggling congregation."

Our vice president was stunned to hear those words. She asked the shopper, "Who said our congregation is small and struggling?"

The shopper replied, "That is the word around town. Why else would you need to have a tag sale?"

It seemed our congregation, just like St. Paul's, had a reputation. At our next council meeting, our vice president shared the conversation she'd had. She then made a motion to have no further tag sales. It passed unanimously.

The truly fascinating thing to me about this experience is that within seven or eight months, we began to have more visitors at worship on Sunday mornings. It was not a deluge but certainly a noticeable trickle. Something had changed. The community's perception of our congregation had changed. Why would anyone want to visit, let alone join, a small struggling congregation? Most wouldn't.

Over the next few years, we continued to make annual increases in the percentage of offering income that we shared. We grew to 18 percent of income. Over the years, we'd become able to provide financial support for some of our local community projects. Just like St. Paul's, the congregation began experiencing growing pains. The worship space was getting more crowded. The Sunday school was overcrowded. I had moved my office out of the church building and into my home. It was suggested that I needed to move back in; I needed to be in our building more. It was generally agreed that we needed to do something.

As our leaders talked about the necessity of building some kind of addition to our present building, they were also well aware that any new building would put added pressure on the church budget. There was strong sentiment that we did not want to decrease the sharing we were doing. It was amazing to watch this congregation make the same decision St. Paul's did when it increased its budget by adding a second pastor. They did not want give up on their sharing. It had become part of who they were.

As is well known, there are two initial phases to any proposed church-building project. In the first phase, you come up with a plan for what you think you need. As you go through this process, usually with an architect, you also begin to get an approximate idea of what the costs will be.

The second phase has to do with raising the necessary funds. We used a fundraising company to help us with this phase. One of the first things their representative did was to walk us through a process called A Look at Our Potential.[3] It is designed to help a congregation determine a conservative indication of the percentage of income currently being contributed by its members. I soon learned that the shorthand term for this was *giving level*.

Once the numbers were all in and the calculations had been made, our fundraiser asked for a meeting with me so he could go over the numbers. He explained that there was some good news and some bad news. The good news was that the giving level in our congregation was 4.5 percent. Most churches he had worked with were less than 2.5 percent. The bad news was that since our people were already giving at such a high level, it didn't seem likely that we'd have the potential to increase our giving enough to cover the cost of the new construction.

Suffice it to say we did go through with the renovation and expansion program. Even after a very successful building-fund campaign, we still wound up with about a $50,000 mortgage. It was not a financial burden to the congregation. We were able to maintain the 18 percent sharing level.

As I stated at the beginning of this chapter, one of the questions I brought with me as I came to this new call was "Could what I experienced at Mt. Holly be carried to another congregation?" The answer was yes. What I didn't know then but learned later was that there were people studying this phenomenon. The term that developed later was *organizational transformation.*

In the March/April 1995 edition of the *Harvard Business Review,* there was an article by John P. Kotter entitled "Leading Change: Why Transformation Efforts Fail." In the article, the author lays out "eight steps to transforming your organization." As I read through that article seven years after I left Turnersville, it was obvious to see how I had unknowingly followed the steps Kotter outlined. It so happened that I was following PC's outline. We'll take a closer look at these eight steps in chapter 6.

Last year, in 2017, I returned to the university that I attended for a homecoming weekend. One of the options offered to returning alums was to hear a presentation by the new athletic director at the university. The rumor was that he was in the processing of turning things around. I wanted to hear what he had to say.

What a surprise! As he began speaking, I quickly realized that he was following John Kotter's playbook. One of the first things he did upon starting in his new position was to spend time talking with faculty and students attempting to discern the culture of the university, particularly as it pertained to its athletic program. Once he had a sense of what was currently going on, he was able to clarify for himself the "preferred future" (vision) for the department. He then went out and visited with some alumni with strong ties to the athletic department. He talked with them about what he had in mind. He was able to recruit some of them to work with him on his board. Then he and his board went to work sharing the new vision they had for the department.

I should note here that the subtitle of the Kotter article was "Why Transformation Efforts Fail." There is no suggestion in his article that this is quick or easy. Indeed, there is no guarantee of success. Certain key elements have to be in place, and the timing has to be right, but it is possible.

It should be noted that what I observed at Mt. Holly and attempted to implement in Turnersville is referred to as a transformational process. It was not simply a matter of getting people on a committee and having few meetings a year to plan a program. We are talking about trying to change the culture of a congregation. This is something quite different from trying to raise some money so the church can pay its bills. We need to acknowledge this at the beginning.

Indeed, it is possible to do stewardship in a congregation. So why don't we? Because it is not that easy! Why not? There are several reasons. I will speak more about these in the next few chapters.

Our first problem is that we are always looking for a quick fix. Secondly, we should not be surprised our people are confused about stewardship. We have seen giving them mixed messages for years. Thirdly, because of the mixed messages, most of our people really do not understand the word *stewardship*. I would suggest we got off track over 1,700 years ago and never got back on.

And finally, if one looks back at the summary that the Ronsvalles provided, one will notice a common theme: money.

- Money is a difficult topic for the church to discuss.
- Attitudes toward money and stewardship require deep changes.

The March, 3, 1993, edition of *Christian Century* included an article by Robert Wuthnow entitled "Pious Materialism: How Americans View Faith and Money."[4] This was followed in 1994 by Wuthnow's book *God and Mammon in America*.[5] In both, Wuthnow explored the tendency of Americans to compartmentalize the economic and religious aspects of their lives.

The unspoken question he raised in both the essay and the book concerned the churches' unwillingness or inability to help its people reflect on the emotional and spiritual power of money in their lives. It is twenty-five years later. We will look at this issue in chapter 7.

CHAPTER THREE

No Quick Fix

The worst thing we can do with a dilemma is to resolve it prematurely because we haven't the courage to live with uncertainty.[1]

—William Sloan Coffin

In the fall of 1996, I attended a one-day event sponsored by the Lutheran churches in the metropolitan New York City area. The title of the event was "Dealing with Stress in the Parish." The leader for the event was Dr. Peter Steinke, author of *Healthy Congregations: A Systems Approach.*[2]

Steinke began by suggesting that clergy experience stress when the people they are working with are anxious. Their people's anxiety triggers reactive behavior.[3] Steinke then went on to list the three most likely triggers of reactive behavior in a congregation: (1) changing a hymnal or liturgy, (2) the death of a child, and (3) anything to do with money.

This third item received universal affirmation from the group. Several clergy shared stories of just how reactive their people became around money issues. Since at that point I was serving on the Stewardship Team of the ELCA and talked about money all of the time, I found this to be, to say the least, a very significant observation.

During the break we had for lunch, I spoke with Steinke further. We both agreed that money was consistently a very anxiety provoking topic. I then asked him, "What suggestions do you give to pastors to help them deal with this anxious behavior around money issues?"

He replied, "No one ever has ever asked me about that."

It was at that point that I decided I needed to learn more about family systems. Steinke suggested that I enroll in the Post Graduate Seminar on Family Emotional Process.[4]

One of the first things I learned is that anxiety in a system, such as a congregation, leads to the following:

1. Reactivity: The vicious cycle of intense reactions of each member to events and to one another.
2. Herding: A process by which the forces for togetherness triumph over the forces of individuality and move everyone to adapt to the least mature members.
3. Blame displacement: An emotional state in which members focus on forces that have victimized them rather than taking responsibility for their own emotional being and destiny.
4. A quick-fix mentality: A low threshold for pain that constantly seeks symptom relief rather than fundamental change.[5]

While all four of these are worthy of further discussion, the one I want to focus on is the quick-fix mentality. I have worked with hundreds of congregations in the area of stewardship and have observed all four of the above. However, the one that is consistently counterproductive to any kind of growth in stewardship is this quick-fix mentality.

As the definition listed above suggests, there is a low threshold for pain. In most congregations, the pain they are experiencing is a financial shortfall of some kind. People get anxious. They want more money, and they want it immediately. I have had hundreds of phone calls that began with, "Our congregation needs help in stewardship. Can you help us?"

I have learned over the years that it is wise to get some further information before I commit to setting up a meeting with some of their leaders. I ask them to describe what they are experiencing and how they think I might be able to help. In almost every case, what they say they are looking for is a stewardship program. When I ask for further clarification, they typically say are looking for a fall program; in other words, a response method. They are looking for a new way to receive pledge cards; a new way that would hopefully promise an increase in both the number of pledges and the amount pledged. In other words, a quick infusion of money.

It should be noted that congregations are not the only ones that behave this way. I was invited in to consult with a group of denominational executives that had determined that their diocese needed to do some work in the area of stewardship. They explained what they saw happening in their churches. They asked me what I had been observing in my work. I told them what I was observing. I shared the "Ronsvalle Summary." They said they thought the Ronsvalles were correct in their summary. They asked for my suggestion as to how they might move forward. I laid out a two-year process in which during the first year, they'd begin working with their clergy. I explained that they would need to be sure their clergy understood what we'd be trying to do as well as the critical role the clergy would need to play in the process.

The group thanked me for my assistance. They asked for a week to consider their options. I received a phone call two days later informing me that they had decided to offer a two-hour workshop in the fall. It was explained that they needed to do something that promised a more immediate return.

In 1993, I was asked to serve on a denominational task force that was to (1) do a careful review of previous stewardship educational programs with the hope that (2) a new resource could be created. The task force looked at programs from across the denominations over several months. Several newly created programs were presented to the task force. Two, in particular, were thought to have promise.

One was a workshop that could be offered on a Saturday morning. The second was a seven-session training event to help inspire and equip stewardship leaders from neighboring congregations. The task force voted to fund the Saturday-morning event. It was thought they might see more immediate results.

More recently, I heard of a denomination that received funding from an insurance company to offer grants to judicatories provided they could come up with a promising new stewardship program. As with most grants, it was assumed that the recipients of the grants would send in progress reports as to how the funds they received were being used. In this instance, six months after the grants were awarded but long before any noticeable changes could be expected, the granting denomination was hoping to see a significant jump in income! It's clear that what they were really looking for was a quick fix.

In 1990, I read Stephen R. Covey's book entitled *Principle-Centered Leadership*.[6] Having spent some of my summers working on a dairy farm, these words really hit home:

> "The only thing that endures over time is the law of the farm: I must prepare the ground, put in the seed, cultivate it, weed it, water it, then gradually nurture growth and development to full maturity. So also, in a marriage or in helping a teenager through a difficult identity crisis—there is no quick fix, where you can just move in and make everything right with a positive mental attitude and a bunch of success formulas. The law of the harvest governs. So, get these principles at the center of your life, at the center of your relationships, at the center of your management contracts, at the center of your entire organization."[7]

Covey is quite clear. There is no quick fix. People familiar with the work of family systems know that Murray Bowen[8] believed it took at least four years to change a family's emotional process. My experience suggests that the same is true for congregations.

Of course, this quick-fix mentality is not limited to churches or organizations. A friend of mine, Ron, works as a personal trainer. It is not at all unusual for people to contact Ron and say something like, "I'm going on vacation, and I would really like to get back in shape."

At that point Ron will ask a few questions. The first one is usually something like "When was the last time you were in shape? When was the last time you were working out on a regular basis?"

Typical answer, "Over five years ago."

Ron will then ask, "When did you want to be in shape? When do plan on going on this vacation?"

Typical response, "In two weeks."

According to friends of mine who are physicians, that same kind of thing happens in their offices, regardless of their specialty. "Doctor, I have this problem, and I need to have you take care of it this morning."

We Christians have options. We don't have to become anxious. Either we can look at our lives as an anxious project of survival, a series of never-ending worries, or we can look at our lives as free gifts sustained in the same mysterious ways as the birds of the air and the lilies of the field. Both options have truth in them. But the fact is that we seem to be better at seeing life as perilous and responding in anxiety and worry than we are as seeing life as a gift and responding with gratitude.[9]

Finally, we are in such a hurry for a quick fix that we don't tend to spend a lot of time intentionally recruiting our stewardship leaders. The makeup of almost all the stewardship committees I've encountered has tended to be three or four people who knew little or nothing about stewardship. They do love their church and were willing to organize a dinner to make sure it receives the money it needs.

When I'd suggested, as I always do, that their stewardship committee needed to spend some time learning more about stewardship ministry, they would politely or not so politely indicate they didn't have time this year. Maybe next year.

According to the biblical witness, Jesus spent months recruiting the disciples and was seemingly very particular about whom he chose. He then took *three years* to prepare them. Why do we keep thinking and acting as if three hours is enough? Obviously, here is one more example of counterproductive behavior when it comes to stewardship.

Why do we keep thinking three hours is enough? Part of the reason, of course, is that we are looking for a quick fix. I think the other reason is that most of our people really don't understand stewardship. That shouldn't surprise us. We in the church haven't always been very clear ourselves.

CHAPTER FOUR

We Got Off Track

*If our religion is based on salvation, our chief emotions
will be fear and trembling. If our religion is based on
wonder, our chief emotion will be gratitude.*

—Carl Jung

It is a well-established fact that, according to the Gospels, Jesus
spoke about money and possessions more than any other topic other
than the kingdom of God. It is also acknowledged that with all of
this talk about money and possessions, we have no examples of Jesus
trying to raise money. In all four Gospels, there is only one reference
to how Jesus's ministry was funded. People "provided for him out of
their resources" (Luke 8:3).

We can read about the earliest Christian communities in the
New Testament. We have Paul's letters and the Gospels. We can read
about an example of early Christian community in the *Didache*.[1]
There are a wide variety of history books covering first century
Christianity and the evolution of the church.

Of what can we be absolutely certain? Not much. We can be
fairly certain that the earliest Christian communities came into being
as a result of Jesus's teaching and preaching to the disciples and their
passing along his message. It was a message about a new way of living, a life with a radical discipline. The kingdom of God is now. God

wants us to live a new way. This new way meant breaking away from the old exclusivity of Judaism. God loves and chooses all people. In response to that love, people were encouraged to live in community with those who understood this new life as they did. The community would provide support for people trying to live this new way. It would also challenge new Christians to mature in their faith (e.g., Ephesians 4:13–15).

The *Didache* describes one kind of community that existed by the year 50 CE. Acts 2:43–47 and Acts 4:32–36 give us other snapshots. People who were part of the Way lived differently. They held all things in common. They shared generously. They took care of each other. There was often a rule (way of living) adopted by the community. If a brother/neighbor is in need, you help. Money and possessions were tools. However, how you used them—allocated them in the community—were matters of life and death. Just ask Ananias and Sapphira (Acts 5). Try to deceive the community about how you are handling your money, and you risked being asked to leave. You will have forsaken the way of life and chosen the way of death (*Didache* 1:1).

For the first three centuries, the people of the Way lived a distinctive lifestyle. There seems to be little doubt that it was a very compelling way to live. Despite experiencing severe persecution from time to time, the early church grew. One might even say exploded. Rodney Stark, in his book *The Rise of Christianity*,[2] lists the following estimates of the number of Christians by fifty-year intervals:

- 100 AD – 8,000
- 150 AD – 40,000
- 200 AD – 200,000
- 250 AD – 1,100,000
- 300 AD – 6,300,000

This growth is not explainable by superior theology. It was the distinctive and compelling way Christians lived.

Then came the conversion of Constantine in 312 AD. Virtually overnight, the church changed. Christianity was no longer persecuted. It was now the preferred religion of the empire. Within a year, the church was receiving financial support from the Roman Empire. Everyone wanted to join the church! The distinctive and disciplined lifestyle had to be greatly relaxed. Example: the church could no longer ask people to spend two years as a catechumen.

Within sixteen years (328 AD), a segment of Christians saw the church losing its core. They longed for that former disciplined community. This is the era of St. Anthony and the Desert Fathers. They would pledge to live by the rule of the community. In 346 AD, St. Pachomius built the first Christian monastery.

However, the vast majority of the church went the way of the world. Everybody was a Christian. There was no longer any distinctive lifestyle. The church was supported by the emperor's taxes. The need for disciplined giving and sharing was lost. From this time on, the Christian faith became the official faith of the Roman Empire, and the Christian Church assumed a magisterial form.

From time to time, era to era, there were those who became very dissatisfied with how the church was living. They called for a new way of living, a distinctive way of living. Often, they placed a stronger emphasis on baptism. In doing so, they often challenged the efficacy of infant baptism. These Anabaptists were perceived to be a threat to the church and the empire and were often burned at the stake (e.g., Jan Hus, 1415).

The funding of the church by the state continued all the way to the Reformation and beyond. The denomination that would be supported in a region of Europe was dependent on the faith of the ruler in the region. Typically, a church tax was imposed by the local government. (*Cuius regio eius religio* is a Latin phrase which literally means "whose realm, his religion," meaning that the religion of the ruler was to dictate the religion of those ruled.) Other offerings were optional.

The Christian church came to America via various waves of immigration. Each group quickly discovered there was no state church. There was no tax system in place to fund the church. The earliest arrivals were not sure what to do. They did realize the church needed funding. Eventually, they devised various ways to fund the church. It was certainly not a cash economy. The church did receive gifts in kind (a chicken, a cow, a load of lumber). This hit-and-miss process gave way to pew rents, fees for services, and church dues.[3] My point is that I think it is significant to notice that the question that early leaders in the American churches asked was not "How are we going to talk about money?" Rather, the question posed was "How are we going to fund the church?"

Notice: Jesus talked about money all of the time. The Ronsvalles noted that the church today is hesitant to do this. Jesus never talked about funding anything. Yet this is the terminology that most churches adopted. The direction was set. The conversation from then on would focus on "How shall we raise the funds we need to support the church?" Basically, how are we going to pay the bills? We created the pay-the-bills mentality the Ronsvalles reported.

Most Protestant churches muddled along paying the bills all the way through the 1860s. It is not until after the Civil War that a noticeable change took place. By 1875 a new term was being used: *systematic benevolence.* Christians realized they needed to move beyond a cow here and a load of wood there. We had to do better than "a little something now and then." We needed to become more regular and systematic in our giving. We needed to develop the habit of weekly giving (offering envelopes). We were encouraged to make a pledge to a cause. We began using subscription lists to get people to commit to underwriting a budget. The YMCA developed these methods, and the church quickly adopted them. This is also the era when church fundraisers (e.g., dinners, sales, shows, concerts) became very popular.

In 1885, a new voice was heard. The man's name was Josiah Strong. The name of his book was *Our Country.*[4] It was an incredibly popular book. In it, Strong observed that the economic changes following the Civil War had changed America and Americans. Instead of helping people better understand the impact of their money on their faith, all the church seemed to say about money was "We need more." Strong was convinced that the church had to do better.

In 1914, Harvey Reeves Calkins wrote an immensely popular book entitled *A Man and His Money.*[5] For the next three years, it sold more copies in the United States than any other book other than the Bible. It had to be reprinted three times. It was in this book that people were introduced to the word *stewardship*. "God is owner, we are stewards." The tithe is a spiritual issue, not a funding issue. Growth in giving is not brought about by pressure from without but a change from within. "Stop talking," said Calkins, "about the needs of the church and begin focusing on what it means to be a steward."

Calkins was an overnight sensation. His denomination, the Methodist-Episcopal Church, hired him to be their secretary for stewardship. They loved what Calkins had to say. However, they did not want to give up on their fundraising practices. The denominational leaders decided they could do both. Calkins argued with these leaders for two years. He was convinced the church should give up fundraising and simply teach stewardship. He was overruled. He resigned in frustration.

Between 1920 and 1950, it would seem that the fundraisers and the stewardship people worked side by side. Both groups wanted what was best for the church. Both groups could quote scripture to prove their case. For Lutherans, a break in this apparent accommodation came in 1956. This was the year that T. A. Kantonen, a professor at Hamma School of Theology, wrote *A Theology for Christian Stewardship*.[6] Kantonen's message was simple and clear. Stop focusing on the needs of the church. Everyone knows the church needs money. If you want to wake people up and transform the church, focus on creating and growing stewards.

Many churches loved Kantonen's theology but were used to their fundraising practices. Recall the Ronsvalles' description of dysfunctional: "The inability to act on one's desires in appropriate ways because of established patterns of counterproductive behavior."[7] Most churches, despite Kantonen's warning, opted to keep doing both; we will talk stewardship and practice fundraising.

In 1982, the Commission on Stewardship of the National Council of Churches published Douglas John Hall's powerful book, *The Steward: A Biblical Symbol Come of Age*.[8] In it, Hall argues that the church needs to stop talking about stewardship as a way to fund itself and focus instead on the symbol of the steward as a way to transform the church. The church loved Hall's book; it sold over five hundred thousand copies. However, most churches seemed committed to doing both.

My observation is that to this day, most churches in the United States are still doing both; they talk stewardship and practice fundraising. The Ronsvalles have shown us that our monetary giving, measured as a percent of our income, has been going down since 1933. This represents eighty years of slow and steady decline. It would seem that trying to do both is not helping. In fact, it has probably been hurting us much more than we've ever imagined.

What happens when you do both? When you talk stewardship and do fundraising, stewardship quickly becomes that which greases the skids, opens the pocketbooks and wallets. Stewardship becomes the fertilizer that increases the yield of the harvest. In other words, stewardship becomes manure.

Shortly after I had started working in the New England area, I met Norris. He was a devoted layman and great steward. One day he happened to ask me, "Did you ever notice that every time you church people talk about stewardship, the next thing that happens is that you put your hand out?"

His comment brought me up short. He wasn't being mean, just describing what he experienced. All too often, that is precisely what happens. Example: we'll begin with some nice words like "Stewardship is not about funding anything; it is about your relationship to your creator." These will be followed by "Now here is your pledge card. The church needs to know how much you are going to give so it can do its budgeting." This is a mixed message. One minute you say stewardship is not about funding the church, and then you turn right around and hand people a pledge card.

Mixed messages are all around us. People are used to encountering them. Initially, people are confused. Then they become angry because it seems like you are trying to fool them. Naturally, they then lose confidence in the person sending the message. In the end, they typically stop listening altogether. Is it any wonder that many church people have stopped listening to stewardship talk?

Several years ago, I was asked to preach at a church on their stewardship Sunday. I was asked to preach on the theme "The Joy of Giving." I focused on the theme that we are the ones who are enriched when we are generous (2 Corinthians 9:11). When I finished my sermon, I sat down.

The pastor then invited the co-chairpersons of their congregation's stewardship committee to come forward and share a few words. The first person proceeded to tell the congregation that if each household could give just 2.4 percent more than they did last year, the congregation would most likely be able to fund their proposed budget for the next year. Then she sat down.

The final speaker, the other stewardship committee co-chair, began with the question, "How many you get your pizza from _____?" He then mentioned the name of the well-known pizza parlor just down the street from the church. He continued, "We all know the price of a pizza. If we all ate one less pizza a week, and none of us need it, we could give the money we save to the church. And *it* needs it." Then he sat down.

On that particular morning, a person sitting in a pew in that church heard three very different messages. Is it any wonder there might have been some confusion about stewardship in the congregation that morning?

I keep encountering churches that do not seem to understand the difference between extrinsic and intrinsic motivation. *Extrinsic* means "not part of the essential nature of someone or something; coming or operating from outside." In terms of one's faith, it refers to "lying outside; not forming a part of or belonging properly to." Extrinsic spiritual beliefs are espoused but not integrated into the personal lives of people. In terms of financial giving, extrinsic motivation will tell me you need to give because your church needs the money.

Intrinsic motivation refers to "belonging to the inmost constitution or essential nature of a thing." Intrinsic beliefs make an observable, measurable difference in daily life. I give because I know I need to. I need to show my gratitude and remind me that I am not the owner. I do what I do because I am who I am.

To this day, most congregations try to do both, appeal to both. This sends a mixed message. It is counterproductive.

Yet one more indicator of the depth of our dysfunction is that we keep applying familiar solutions to our problems; we stick to what we know best. I keep watching church bodies receive less and less offering income. So what do they do? Typically, a decision is made to have some kind of a one-time special appeal to cover a deficit. And what happens if the one-time special appeal works? They have another one the next year. And if it works again? They make it an annual appeal.

Pushing harder and harder on familiar solutions while the fundamental problems persist or worsen is a reliable indicator of nonsystematic thinking—what we often call the "what we need is a bigger hammer" syndrome. The long-term, most insidious consequence of applying nonsystematic solutions is increased need for more and more of the solution.[9]

One hundred years ago, Harvey Reeves Calkins told the church to stop focusing on funding and start focusing on creating stewards. The church refused to listen. Fifty years later, T. A. Kantonen said the same thing. Again, no one was ready to listen. In the 1990s, the number of voices calling for a change grew noticeably. Douglas John Hall says, "Stewardship, even in the congregation and even at the level of basic finances, must from now on find its rationale at the heart of the faith, an essential aspect of belief: part of the end-purpose, and not merely a means to some ill-defined and nebulous spiritual goal."[10]

In 1992, Dean R. Hoge and Douglas L. Griffin wrote *Research on Factors Influencing Giving to Religious Bodies*.[11] In it, they stated, "We teach stewardship and we practice fundraising… Is it any wonder that two-thirds of the lay people who we interviewed said that stewardship education materials had no effect on their level of giving."

In 1996, John and Sylvia Ronsvalle wrote *Behind the Stained Glass Windows: Money Dynamics in the Church*.[12] They again observed, "We are sending mixed signals." We need to get the focus away from fundraising and in the direction of stewardship.

In 1998, Loren B Mead said in *Financial Meltdown in the Mainline?*[13], "We have made stewardship a euphemism for fundraising and confused everyone."

In 1999, William Avery, professor of stewardship at the Lutheran Theological Seminary at Gettysburg, wrote, "For stewardship to have meaning in the church again we need to do one specific thing. We have to separate stewardship from fundraising. We have to separate stewardship from its direct connection to the annual budget."[14]

Dr. Martin Marty was quoted in the 1999 edition of *Giving, saying,* "My main contention is that while it may be giving, it is not stewardship if it is focused on yield, on the year's returns, or on the strategic planned-for-need of an institution."[15]

Clearly, voice after voice was saying the same thing; stop trying to do stewardship and fundraising at the same time. The problem was that no one suggested how this shift was supposed to happen. Was that up to the local pastor? The local stewardship committee? What would that new approach look like?

It should also be acknowledged that it was precisely during the 1990s that many congregations were struggling financially. In 1997, Robert Wuthnow's excellent book *The Crisis in the Churches: Spiritual Malaise, Fiscal Woe*[16] pointed correctly to what was happening in many of our churches. Unfortunately, the changes that Wuthnow called for came at a time when many congregations were so worried about just surviving. They were not able to listen. Many kept hoping for a quick fix.

Two thousand eight saw the publishing of *Passing the Plate: Why American Christians Don't Give Away More Money* by Christian Smith and Michael O. Emerson.[17] The authors of this book are not theologians but sociologists. They do not comment on whether Christians should be more generous. Their focus is on why they seem to not be. In essence, their observation is that American Christians behave exactly like all other Americans. On the whole, there is nothing distinctive in how they live and certainly not in their giving.

It was noted previously in this chapter that during its first 300 years, the church grew remarkably. This growth is not explainable by superior theology. It was the distinctive and compelling way Christians lived.

If one moves to the end of *Passing the Plate*, the authors offer a list of how to begin to address the current situation. Their number one suggestion is: the church needs to move away from the "pay the bills" mentality it has instilled in its members. We need to move in the direction of helping our people live the vision of what they say God calls them to be.[18]

What is this vision? It's time to take a look.

CHAPTER FIVE

Back on Track

*Unless Christ has priority in the life of a church member, he
or she may be persuaded to support the church but will never
be a mature Christian steward. Thus, the main problem in
the financial support of the church is not getting deeper into
people's pocketbooks, but getting Christ into people's hearts.*

—T. A. Kantonen[1]

Several years ago, I met with a church council from a congregation
in Brooklyn, New York. It was a Saturday morning. The council was
concerned about the cash flow in the congregation and invited me in
for a conversation. After a few pleasantries, we got to the heart of the
matter. Offerings were not keeping up with expenses. They all hoped
I could give them an answer that morning.

I asked the group if their congregation had a stewardship committee and how that committee understood its ministry. I was told
there used to be one. It was at that point that one of members of the
council interrupted the conversation and said, "I know what is going
on here. Our people aren't giving because they aren't aware of our
needs. People don't think the church needs money."

I asked the rest of the leaders if they agreed. They were not
sure. So I proposed an experiment. The congregation was located on
Fourth Avenue. It was a busy Saturday morning. Many people were

walking up and down the street. I invited the council to watch from a distance.

We all went outside. I waited for a couple to come walking down the street. I stopped them and asked if I could ask them two very simple questions. They agreed. The first question I asked them was, "Do you know what kind of building this is?" I then pointed to the church building.

The man said, "That is a church."

I said, "Correct." I then asked my second question, "Do you think that church needs money to run?"

The woman said yes. I thanked the couple for their help. I had this same conversation several times. The answers were always the same. I then turned to the council who were huddled about forty feet away and said, "There you have it. Everyone walking down this street knows the church needs money."

The logic seems clear: if funding the church is a matter of common sense ($A = B$) and stewardship is concerned with funding the church ($C = A$), then stewardship must be a matter of common sense ($C = B$).

In 1920, Harvey Reeves Calkins wrote, "Stewardship is not a natural human conception. The unaided human instinct will not discover it. The recognition of stewardship marks the supremacy of spiritual man. It begins with the acknowledgement of God as owner, for human stewardship is the necessary correlate of divine ownership."[2]

To summarize, on the one hand, we have talked as if stewardship is a matter of common sense; everyone knows the church needs funding. And then we also say stewardship is not a natural human conception; it is *not* simply a matter of common sense. How can it be both a matter of common sense and not a matter of common sense? This is a classic mixed message. The church has been talking this way for almost a hundred years. No wonder church people have, for the most part, stopped listening to stewardship talk. No wonder our giving levels have been decreasing since 1933. It seems this would be a good time to gain some clarity on this word *stewardship*.

The New Testament word that we translate as *stewardship*, *oikonomia*, conveys at least two different meanings. In Ephesians 1:9–

10, "[God] has made known to us the mystery of his will, according to his good pleasure that he set forth in Christ, as an oikonomia for the fullness of time." In the New Revised Standard Version translation of this text, *oikonomia* is translated as *plan*. The word *stewardship* in this text refers to the plan that God has for all creation, namely, that all of life would come together and experience the peace and unity God intended from the beginning of time. This use of *oikonomia* seems to have little or no connection to church funding.

Luke 16:1–2 also contains this word *oikonomia*. "There was a rich man who had a manager, and charges were brought to him that this man was squandering his property. So, he summoned him and said to him, 'What is this I hear about you? Give me an account of your oikonomia.'" The NRSV translation of *oikonomia* in this text is *management*. Is this an oblique reference to church funding? It does not seem to be. Nor is it immediately clear how this second use of *oikonomia* (*management*) has any connection to the first (God's plan).

It has been my experience that a helpful way to gain some clarity at this point is to take the English word *stewardship* and break it into its component parts, i.e., *steward* + *ship*. The word *ship* in this instance is not a reference to anything naval or nautical. Nor is it a reference to a shipping company, e.g., Federal Express. *Ship*, in this instance, is a suffix that refers to attitudes and actions consistent with the preceding noun. *Stewardship* refers to attitudes and actions consistent with being a steward.

This word *steward* can also be confusing. In my conversations with groups over the years, the most immediate connection some people make is with men who work on ships. Others remember when a female flight attendant was called a stewardess. When I've asked people for a job description for a steward, they usually suggest terms like *caretaker* or *manager*. While both of these are basically correct, I think we gain deeper insight if we return to the Greek word for *steward*, *oikonomos*.

Again, I think it is helpful to break this word down into its constituting roots *oikos* and *nomos*. The word *oikos* can be translated as *house* or *household*. The image I find more helpful is that of a farm. A farm is made up of much more than a farmhouse. There are barns, sheds, silos, and holding areas. There can be animals, machinery, fields, orchards, and a supply of water.

To this image of an *oikos*, we add the word *nomos*. In this instance *nomos* is not a reference to a rule or a law but is a derivative of the verb *nemein*,[3] "to manage or administer." Putting the two pieces back together, we have *oikonomos*, a word that combines the ideas of *household* and *management*. The important thing to keep in mind is that this word *oikonomos* is a noun, not a verb. *Oikonomos* is not the Greek word for the management of a household but rather the title given to a servant in the household. I think it is also significant to note that *oikonomos* conveys not only a certain title within the household but also a job description.

There is one more important piece here that is so obvious that it is often overlooked. An *oikonomos*/steward is not the owner or the master of the household, but a servant who manages the household. A steward is to exercise their management in keeping with the intentions of the owner. The underlying assumption is that the owner/master of the household has already established a plan for this management. When the steward is placed in charge of the household, it is a foregone conclusion that the steward is not free to do as he/she pleases. A steward is not their own boss.

At first, this observation may not appear to be very significant. One way of demonstrating its deeper significance is by considering what it would mean to be, if you will, the opposite of an *oikonomos*. An *oikonomos* manages a household according to the scheme of the owner. The opposite would be an *autos-nomos*, someone who manages based on a scheme they devised themselves. Notice the subtle but profound difference. The *oikonomos*, by the very nature of his self-understanding, is accountable to the owner. The *autonomos* is precisely that, autonomous, accountable only to himself.

John C. Haughey, author of *Virtue and Affluence*, summarizes it this way: "An autonomous steward is a contradiction in terms. You can't be managing the Master's property as a steward and living a heart life, a mind life, a norm life independently of the Master. A *sarx*-directed steward, one who seeks to be self-sufficient and self-reliant, won't be a steward very long because he'll be interested in making his own way."[4]

We are now at, what I think, is the critical point of any discussion of stewardship. We have determined that stewardship has to do with the attitudes and actions of a steward. The next thing we need to acknowledge is that most people, based on the words they use and the actions we can observe, do not understand themselves as stewards. For me, this means that before we can start looking at stewardship as "God's plan for the fullness of time" or begin to talk about stewardship as "managing one's life and possessions in keeping with the mind of the Master," we need to look at the whole issue of attitude. Or, as Luke T. Jonson calls it, self-disposition.

> In spite of the multiplicity of mandates, the basic perception of the Old Testament as a whole regarding possessions is quite clear and straightforward—material things are important as signs of our self-disposition. If we recognize that we and all that we have are gifts from God, we will respond to his covenant with justice and care for our fellow humans. If we refuse to acknowledge this dependence on God, we will make an idol of possessions and do evil to our fellow humans in order to gain ascendency over them.[5]

It has been my experience that when people hear the word *stewardship*, they associate the word with something that one *does* with one's possessions. I am suggesting that in dealing with possessions, the first thing one needs to learn is how to *be* with them rather than what to *do* with them. If stewardship is a matter of attitude and action, then seemingly we need to look first at that attitude!

What is the attitude/mind-set of a steward? What does it mean to say that I understand myself as a steward? I think it begins with the understanding that (1) there is a God and (2) it is not me. God is the creator; I am the creature. The steward, the *oikonomos*, looks at all they have and declares, "All of this stuff of life has been placed in my hands by God. I do not own any of this; God is the owner. I do possess it for a time and need to manage it according to the purposes that God has in mind."

Over against this mind-set, the *autonomos* looks at all he has and declares or at least subconsciously assumes, "All that I have is mine. I earned it. I own it. I am free to do with it as I choose."

There is a marvelous depiction of this difference in attitude in the Old Testament book of Deuteronomy, chapter 8. In this chapter, Moses is speaking to the people of Israel as they are about to enter the Promised Land. It is a classic "good news/bad news" story. The good news was that the people were going to enter a land that would provide them with all they were hoping for. The people listening to Moses had to be excited by all they were about to receive. That was the good news. The bad news was that with all of the abundance that God would be providing, Moses was worried that the people might begin taking it for granted. The temptation of wealth and prosperity is spiritual amnesia.[6]

Some years ago, I attended an event at Union Theological Seminary in New York City. The presenter was Dr. Walter Brueggemann. At the end of his third presentation, Brueggemann said, "At the risk of making it sound too simplistic, I think the entire Old Testament can be summarized in one question: 'Will you remember or will you forget?'"[7]

In Deuteronomy 8: 17–19, Moses warns the people of Israel: "Do not say to yourself, 'My power and the might of my own hand have gotten me this wealth… If you forget the Lord your God and follow other gods…you shall surely perish.'" Remember and live. Forget and die.

Moses was very clear. Remembering is critical. Eighteen chapters later, in Deuteronomy 26, Moses offers a suggestion as to how the people of Israel could remind themselves so that they did not forget. "When you have come into the land that the Lord your God is giving as an inheritance to possess [not own!]…you shall take the first of all the fruit of the ground…that the Lord your God is giving you…and put it in a basket… You shall go to the priest…and say 'So now I bring the first of the fruit of the ground that you, O Lord, have given me'" (Deuteronomy 26:1–3).

For all the people who were convinced that stewardship had something to do with giving, you were right! But the issue here is not funding anything. It is about my need to give, my need to give out of a sense of deep gratitude, and my need to remind myself that I am not the owner, only a steward.

Earlier in this chapter, I quoted Calkins: "Stewardship is not a natural human conception. The unaided human instinct will not discover it." If Calkins is correct and I think he is, then how does one develop this unnatural way of seeing the world? My experience has been that this does not come as the result of reading a book; it involves a process of transformation.

The first words spoken by Jesus in the earliest of four Gospels, Mark, are these, "Time's up! God's Kingdom is here. Change your mind and live this message."[8] Jesus's announcement was more than sharing of some interesting information. It was a call to people to begin thinking and living a new way.

Paul speaks of this new way of living in Romans 12:1–2. "I appeal to you therefore, my brothers and sisters, by the mercies of God, to present your bodies as a living sacrifice, holy and acceptable to God, which is your spiritual worship. Do not be conformed but transformed by the renewing of your mind so that you may discern what is the will of God—what is good and acceptable and perfect."[9]

How does one experience this transformation? From what I have seen, we are not talking about a one-time event, but rather about a life-long process. I offer Saul as an example. We know he had a personal experience on road to Damascus (see Acts 9:1–18), but that was not the end, only the beginning. We also know that it took three years (see Galatians 1:18) of thinking and talking with others before Saul, now Paul, went to Jerusalem.

In Matthew 4:18, we hear Jesus's invitation: "Follow me." The earliest followers of Jesus were his disciples. The very word *disciple* suggests people who were preparing themselves to live a certain discipline, a new way of living. To be a follower of Jesus means that His mind, His way of doing things, His norms, and His way of operating would become one's way of thinking and living. This conversion, this *becoming*, is a never-ending process.

My conversion did not happen on a highway, but in a living room. It began as a brother in Christ shared with me his story of how he came to understand himself as a steward. It was followed by hearing other similar stories. It was those stories that planted the seeds that would later germinate. What began for me as simply an inspiring story slowly became something that excited me; it was enticing. I wanted to experience what they experienced. It is my sense that this is what happened in the early church. People not part of a Christian community observed these people living differently—living joyfully—even in the midst of persecution. It was very attractive.

It should be becoming rather obvious by now that when we talk of stewardship ministry in this way, it is *very different* from four well-intentioned people planning a dinner to raise funds for a congregation. It is a ministry that, at its core, invites people to "not be conformed…but be transformed by the renewing of their minds." Stewardship ministry is transformational ministry. The world tells us we are owners. We understand ourselves as stewards, accountable to God, the owner. Have we in the church been saying this clearly in the past? I'm not so sure.

What should also be becoming obvious is that serving on a stewardship committee in a congregation should be quite different from the other committees. Example: you can serve on property or finance committee and not expect your life to be transformed. However, this is the goal of stewardship ministry. The fact that this is the case and has rarely, if ever, been acknowledged is yet one more example of our counterproductive behavior.

I recently visited a congregation that I knew at one time had had a strong stewardship program. Apparently, things had changed. I was invited in for a conversation. It did not take long to figure out that the current stewardship leaders had not been carefully selected. While they were very well-intentioned, they did not understand stewardship ministry. Why was that so bad? Because if you put uncommitted stewards to lead the stewardship committee, the problem is not simply that they might only do a modest job. Too often, they unknowingly *undo* any previous good work that was done.

Over the last twenty years, author after author has written about the churches' need to move away from a "pay the bills" mentality and toward a "live the vision" mentality.[10] It is my sense Hall spelled out his "vision" in *The Steward*:

> Stewardship, even in the congregation and even at the level basic finances, must from now on find its rationale at the heart of the faith, an essential aspect of belief: part of the end-purpose, and not merely a means to some ill-defined and nebulous spiritual goal… We have buried this treasure in the financial departments of our churches, and have so domesticated the biblical concept that we have lost sight of its truly radical implications… What we have been harboring in our midst [hiding under our collection plates!] is in fact a pearl of great price. Our task is the elevation, and enlarging of the stewardship concept.[11]

How do we make this transition from "pay the bills" to "live the vision"? One congregation at a time! This is not something a denominational office can mandate. Nor is it a process that is quick, easy, or automatic. John Kotter, in his article "Leading Change: Why Transformation Efforts Fail,"[12] makes it very clear: transformation efforts often fail.

In chapter 1, I described how this process seemed to work in Mt. Holly. In chapter 2, I described how I introduced this new way of doing stewardship in Turnersville. I have observed other congregations that have successfully made this transition. I have observed others, and led others, that failed. I have learned a lot as I experienced both the successes and the failures.

CHAPTER SIX

Step by Step

*Christianity must mean everything to us before
it can mean anything to anyone else.*

—Donald Soper

I wrote in the introduction that I don't think we should give upon this idea of stewardship. I hesitate to refer to what I have been describing as new stewardship. Obviously, it is not new. The image of the steward comes out of the Old Testament. Calkins began describing this way of thinking and living in 1914. I haven't met anyone who has read Hall's *The Steward* who was not struck by both the power and the timeliness of his writing. The problem I have been attempting to address is our inability to move from theology to practice. Why has it been so difficult to take this new concept of stewardship and move it into our congregations?

Of course, the answer is simple. We are talking about change, significant change. The title of John Kotter's article is "Leading Change." In this chapter, I want to describe a process for introducing this new stewardship into the life of a congregation. I am going to use Kotter's "Eight Steps to Transforming Your Organization" as a way of providing some order.

Here are John Kotter's eight steps:

1. Establishing a Sense of Urgency
2. Forming a Powerful Guiding Coalition
3. Creating a Vision
4. Communicating the Vision
5. Empowering Others to Act on the Vision
6. Planning for and Creating Short-Term Wins
7. Consolidating Improvements and Producing Still More Change
8. Institutionalizing New Approaches

1. Establishing a Sense of Urgency

One of the first things I learned as I began to study family systems is that systems (families, organizations, churches) do not like to change. They will resist change; they will fight change. They like to stay just the way they are. Anyone who has been around churches for any length time has experienced this. One thing that might get a congregation to be more open to change is if it realizes that it may soon need to close. I specifically used the word *might* because I have worked with churches that refused to change even as their lights were turned off for the last time.

When I began my ministry in Turnersville, I did not have to establish a sense of urgency. It was already there. The leaders in the congregation were seriously wondering if their congregation would survive. They weren't thinking in terms of introducing a new way of looking at stewardship. They were just trying to keep going. Their willingness to "try anything at this point" gave me an open door.

This was not the case when PC came to Mt. Holly; survival was not an issue. The urgency in Mt. Holly was supplied by PC. He came with an agenda; he came with a vision of what stewardship ministry could look like in a congregation. Somewhere along the way, he had caught the virus. In my work with congregations over the years, this has been a critical piece; someone has to have caught the virus. Then, too, this virus was most likely not acquired from reading a book. This virus is usually caught from another person who has the virus. I have found it to be quite contagious.

Dr. Ed Friedman was fond of saying, "Transformation occurs when one person begins acting differently." This is how the change begins in a congregation; one person begins acting differently. I have never encountered a person who advocated seeing stewardship in this new way who had not already caught the virus. My experience is that the opposite is also true. Unless someone in your organization has caught the virus, there is little chance of infecting others.

I also need to make it clear here that simply being in financial trouble is not the kind of urgency Kotter is referring to. Congregations who see themselves as struggling to survive are often not ready to learn. Their anxiety will have them looking for a quick fix. The leaders in Turnersville were looking for precisely this when I arrived. Fortunately, I wasn't.

2. Forming a Powerful Guiding Coalition

Over the years, I have received innumerable phone calls from pastors looking for help in stewardship. When I receive this kind of call, I usually ask a few questions. First, "Where did you learn about stewardship, and what did you learn?" If one listens closely, it is pretty easy to figure out if the caller is talking about raising money for the church or creating stewards. As I indicated earlier, most of the time, the callers were looking for assistance with their fall program. When this was the case, I was happy to suggest a couple of places they might look.[1]

If it sounded to me that the caller was looking for more than a fall program and that they had some sense of this new understanding of stewardship, I would then ask, "Do you have a stewardship committee in place?" If the answer to that question was no, I would typically respond, "That's good."

They would often ask, "Why is that good?" I'd then explain that having an old stewardship committee in place was often more of a hindrance. In most of the cases, I encountered the old committee typically understood their task to be running a fall campaign. When people are deeply ingrained in that old mind-set and the old way of doing things, it is very hard to get them to change. Again, we are looking at what the Ronsvalles described as "established patterns of counterproductive behavior." It is usually better, in the long run, to have to recruit a new committee. It will take some time up front, but it is better than continually experiencing the resistance that the old committee will typically offer.

In a couple of instances, I worked with congregations where a newly arriving pastor was deeply committed to helping their congregations embrace this new understanding of stewardship. The problem they encountered was an old committee that was deeply entrenched in doing what they had always done. Both pastors were smart enough to realize it would not be wise to simply fire the old committee. So what did they do?

In slightly different ways, they decided to create a new committee. They let the old committee remain as the stewardship committee. That group continued to organize a dinner in the fall and order the offering envelopes. They then, through a process of visitation and conversation, recruited a new committee that became their guiding coalition.

The critical factor to keep in mind is that no one person can transform an organization; this includes churches. I often remind pastors that Jesus did not work alone. One of the first things Jesus did as his public ministry began was to identify and recruit the disciples to work with him. The recruitment method he used did not include standing on a street corner in Capernaum and shouting, "Does anyone want to become one of my disciples?"

Instead, Jesus spoke to people one-on-one (Mt. 9:9). He told them they would need to leave their old life behind (Mark 1:16–20). He told them it was not going to be easy (Mt. 8:20). He also promised that this new life was well worth the commitment (John 10:10). Jesus was also clear with his early disciples that they would need to follow him around for a while so they could watch and learn.

If you are going to put together a guiding coalition, you need to be clear with them what you are trying to do and why. You must be able to use the word *transformation* and not have people running for the doors. If you are not able to convince this group that what you have in mind is worth doing, you need to stop. If you can't convince the people you handpicked, you have little chance of convincing anyone else.

The other important piece of Kotter's advice is that this group needs to include at least one person (preferably more than one) that is already a recognized leader in the congregation. This person (or persons) may not be on your governing board at the moment. They do need to be one of a handful of people your congregation looks to for leadership. If you don't know who those people are, you need to stop. It is possible you have no real leaders in your congregation. I have seen this. You still need to stop and begin the process of identifying and equipping some leaders. Without leaders, organizations will die.

Another possibility is that there are leaders, but you don't recognize who they are. When pastors have said this, I recommended that they have some one-on-one conversations with the members of their current governing board. Ask each of them who they think the leaders are and why they think so. Do not debate the names that are mentioned—simply make a note. After talking with five or six people, look at your notes. Were there any names that came up two or three times?

Another question I have found revealing when I talk with people is, "Who is the spiritual leader of this congregation?" I also make it clear, they cannot say the pastor. It has to be someone other than the pastor. When you hear the same name mentioned four or five times, you have a leader. They may not be an officer in your congregation or chair a committee, but people clearly respect what they have to say.

Another factor I think pastors need to be aware of is that group of two or three households that give the largest offerings. I know from experience that as soon as I say this, some people are going to balk. One of the constant fears I hear pastors express is that they do not want to know who the largest financial givers are, so they cannot be accused of giving anyone preferential treatment. I am not suggesting any kind of preferential treatment. I am simply acknowledging that most congregations have at least one or two households that are currently providing more financial support to the church than the average household.

I'll take it a step further and suggest that your other members probably have some awareness (despite our saying that all giving is confidential) of who these people are. Mrs. Smith or Mr. Jones may not be thought of as leaders in your congregation, but they most likely are perceived as people of influence. If you are trying to put together a powerful guiding coalition, it would be unwise to not keep them in mind. To be clear, I am not insinuating you need to get their permission. I am saying that if they support your change efforts, if not actually serve on your team, it can be very helpful.

In summary, it is in this step that I have observed most efforts at leading change in a congregation fail. You dare not skip this step. Time spent pulling together the right group of people is time well spent. You are building the foundation from which you will grow. If your situation is typical, there will be pressure to get the group up and running. Take your time.

3. Creating a Vision

In the situation we are describing, namely, introducing a new understanding of stewardship in a congregation, we don't have to create an entirely new vision. In Hall's book, for example, he lays out his vision of the direction in which we could be moving. Your goal is to be familiar enough with his (or yours or some other) vision that your team can adapt it to your situation and make it your own.

When I arrived in Turnersville, I did not have Hall's book. Even if I had, that would not have been the place to start. I knew that the members of our team needed to learn more about stewardship. I also knew that along the way, we'd be looking at money and giving and that these are emotionally charged issues. I knew we had to begin by doing some relationship building. We needed to get to know each other. We needed to be able to trust each other.

With this in mind, I had our team spend about half of our time together during those first six months getting to know each other. The other half, as I mentioned in chapter 2, we'd spend reading a stewardship-related article or essay. Reading these articles helped everyone become more familiar with stewardship theology, terminology, and practice. It was also very important and beneficial to discuss them as a group. Today, after a few months, the team could read, for example, *Giving to God*, and take Powell's insights and slowly but surely incorporate them into their own lives as well as the life of the congregation. However, don't start with a book; start with building relationships.

The process we are engaging in is not simply about disseminating information. It is also attempting to internalize it. We are not just talking about way of thinking but also a way of living. We are not just talking about a vision we would eventually share with the congregation, but we are also reflecting on how we will live that vision in our daily lives. It is in this step that St. Paul's invitation to be transformed (Romans 12:2) begins taking place. It is here that the virus is transmitted.

Again, this is not a process you want to rush. Remember, "the only thing that endures over time is the law of the farm."[2] First, you prepare the ground (carefully select the people you want on the team). Then you plant the seed. However, you don't plant a seed and expect a harvest the next week. There needs to be time for the seed to germinate. The soil needs to be cultivated, weeded, and watered. The growth needs to be nurtured.

4. Communicating the Vision

You now have a group (guiding coalition) in place that is talking about changing the way the congregation does stewardship ministry. While I am in no way advocating secrecy, I would not say too much about what this group is doing until the members of the group have had time to do some clarifying among themselves. This can take up to a year or more. Once the group has agreed on their vision, you will want to begin to share what you have learned with the rest of the congregation. An obvious place to begin would be with the governing board/parish council. Keep your elected leaders informed of your conversations. Be ready to answer any questions that may arise.

It would also be helpful to let the entire congregation know what your committee/team has been talking about and why. You could include a written report in your parish newsletter. That being said, my experience has been that the most powerful communication takes place as the members of your team share their stories with other members of the congregation. Their excitement and their passion will be infectious.

5. Empowering Others to Act on the Vision

After about a year of meeting together, your typical team will have a pretty clear idea of the direction in which they want to move. While there will always be ongoing teaching and learning, the team should have an idea of an initial action step they could suggest to the congregation. It would be most helpful if this step will (1) serve as a teaching moment/experience, (2) involve as much of the congregation as possible, (3) not involve any major change (e.g., rewriting your constitution, restructuring your congregation, changing the budget process).

An option that I suggest to congregations is to have them calculate their level of giving.[3] There are several reasons why this is a very helpful exercise. First, it gives you a starting point for future comparison. This is important because down the road, you will want to be able to measure/evaluate if this new stewardship is, in fact, having a positive impact. Recall that the Ronsvalles noted that while the total number of dollars given was increasing, these dollars represented a smaller percentage of household income. It is important to know the giving level of your congregation as you begin, i.e., to establish a benchmark.

You can do the calculation on a yearly basis. However, it is also important to keep in mind that this number will most likely not change dramatically from year to year. Don't expect to grow from 1.5 percent to 2.5 percent in one year. Growing from a giving level of 1.5 percent to 1.6 percent is significant growth that needs to be celebrated.

Please note that this is a subtle but significant change in thinking. In the past, if you asked most congregations whether they had a good year in stewardship, the reference point they would typically look at is "Did we pay our bills?" This reinforces the "pay the bills" mentality. If we are trying to help our people move away from paying the bills toward living the vision, we will want to evaluate our progress accordingly; i.e., was there a change in giving level?

The other very significant factor in doing the giving-level calculation is that it requires the congregation to come up with a number that represents the annual household income in your congregation. There are several ways to determine this figure. One option is to talk to a local real estate broker and ask them what the minimum household income one would need to be in order to purchase a home in your area. A second option would be to look up the federal income statistics for your ZIP code. The most accurate way is to do an anonymous income survey in your congregation. Needless to say, this third option tends to make people the most anxious.

As we know, using a term like *income* means we will be talking about money. We know money talk can trigger all sorts of anxious reactivity. The purpose here is not to go out of our way to agitate people. Rather, in knowing that some people will get agitated, we will want to assess how agitated they become. I have worked with congregations that have refused to do this calculation. This kind of reactivity around money usually means you will want to move forward very slowly.

6. Planning for and Creating Short-Term Wins

Basically, what Kotter is referring to is making sure that you can let your congregation know that you are making progress. In the case of Turnersville, it was making it through 1978 in the black. We did not declare total victory, but we did recognize a significant first step. We had a short-term win we could announce and celebrate.

If your initial action step was doing a giving-level calculation and you chose to do an income survey, then celebrate the fact that the council and congregation agreed it was an important thing to do. You can report the number of households that participated in the income survey. The more households that participated, the greater reason to declare a win.

I would also be the first to acknowledge that a lot comes down to how you spin the data. I don't mean lie. I mean accentuate. Example: Let's assume that you do this calculation, and the number you come up with is 1.5 percent. Depending what part of the country you live in, that is a pretty low number. You have at least two options in reporting that number.

Option one: You can report that this is a low number that reflects some unhealthy giving patterns. You could even take it a step further and berate the congregation for this bad number.

Option two: You can report the 1.5 percent number and indicate this is not a good number. You could then continue, "With a giving level this low, we continue to stay alive. Imagine what we could accomplish if we ever tapped into the resources we have available!"

At first glance, this second option may not sound too exciting. What we need to keep in mind is that most struggling congregations tend to live with the mantra "we just don't have enough." This 1.5 percent number indicates there is plenty of money in the congregation. People may not be giving it, but it is there. God has given us all that we need. Our scarcity talk needs to stop.

7. Consolidating Improvements and Producing Still More Change

This stage of the process could look quite different from congregation to congregation. We are probably about four or five years into the process. Some congregations may have made changes to their budgeting process, e.g., unified vs non-unified budgets. I've observed congregations that made significant changes to their offering procedures. In the examples I cited in chapters 1 and 2, the congregations focused on giving beyond themselves, e.g., providing funding for community projects.

8. Institutionalizing New Approaches

Once again, this could take various forms depending on the congregation. One of the more exciting examples that I've observed took place at the congregation I mentioned in chapter 1, St. Paul's. Several years after I had left, the congregation made some very significant decisions. One of these was to *not* have an endowment fund.

As I mentioned in chapter 1, one of the things that the pastor prior to PC had done was to teach his people to love the church. He spoke openly about the importance of having a will and including the church in that will. About twenty years later, the congregation began receiving a number of bequests. If the bequest had certain designation, these were honored. In this case, those gifts went into a memorial fund. However, the memorial fund established a policy that all designated gifts had to be used for that purpose within a year. If after a year, nothing had been done, the designated gift lost its designated status. The congregation did not want to see its memorial fund be filled with money that could not be used for others.

If there was no direction given, the financial bequests went into a building fund. As one can imagine, the building fund began to grow. Since a new building had been completed in 1965 and was paid for, the congregation's leadership did not want to have more and more money simply accumulating in the building fund and not be available to help others (blessed to be a blessing).

It was at that point that the congregation decided to set a limit on the amount of money that could accumulate in the building fund. However, they did not want set a figure and be locked into that number forever. So they decided to change the name and the purpose of the account to the Building Emergency Fund. The funds in this account would be available if "the roof blew off or the furnace blew up." The Building Emergency Fund could accumulate funds to a dollar figure not to exceed the annual budget of the congregation for the previous year.

Once the Building Emergency Fund reached this limit, all funds beyond this were transferred into the Seminary Fund. The Seminary Fund originally made it possible for the congregation to provide scholarships to members of the congregation who chose to attend seminary. It did help several members attend seminary. At this stage, the interest from the Seminary Fund can cover the tuition, room, and board for two students. St. Paul's continues to own and manage the Seminary Fund. The recommendations as to who receives the scholarships are made by the seminary with whom they are affiliated.

What I have attempted to show is that congregations can do amazing things once they catch the virus. As Jesus so boldly promised, "Give, and it will be given to you. A good measure...running over, will be put in your lap" (Luke 6:38).

It should be obvious by now that what I have been describing is something way beyond teaching people about stewardship. The goal of the process is creating stewards. It is important to keep in mind that while personal growth is challenging work, it can also be very exciting and very energizing. It is this excitement and energy that keeps the process moving.

There is one more significant factor that I want to address. I'll begin with a story. One evening I was asked to meet with a church's governing board. They said they wanted to talk with me about stewardship. As we began the meeting, the board wanted to make sure that I was aware of what they were already doing. Their pastor began. He said that he spoke about tithing often during his sermons. He gave witness to the fact that he thought it was an important Christian discipline. His board nodded in affirmation.

Their stewardship chairperson spoke next. She spoke about all of the ways that she used to inform her congregation of where their offerings went. She made oral announcements at worship services, put informative inserts in their worship bulletins, and wrote articles for their newsletter. The board members once again nodded in agreement.

The president of the board then looked at me and asked, "Given everything you have heard we are doing, why aren't our people giving more?"

I then explained to the group that there are three areas to consider when we are talking about giving: how I give, where I give, and why I give. "Your pastor spoke about tithing. That is how I give. Marilyn spoke about where I give. Who is addressing the most critical of those three: why I give?"

One of my favorite stewardship-related books in Mark Allan Powell's *Giving to God: The Bible's Good News about Living a Generous Life*. In the book, Powell does a fabulous job of describing our giving as an act of worship. In the very first chapter, he makes the point that "Our principal concern in giving should not be in where we give, or how we give, or how much we give. First let us focus on the *why*. If we give with hearts that have been touched with God's love, if we give with hearts full of devotion for the God who loves us, then the question of *where* and *how* and *how much* will work themselves out."[4]

I absolutely agree. One of the changes that people often identify as they are in the process is a distinct change in motivation; there is a shift from external to internal motivation. St. Paul refers to this distinction when he encourages the Corinthians to see their offering as "voluntary gifts and not extortions" (2 Cor. 9:5). Why is this so significant? There is a huge difference between external and internal motivation.[5]

Here is yet another critical place where the church has been guilty of counterproductive behavior. Instead of recognizing this difference and helping our people to be internally motivated in their giving, we continue to present the church as one more organization that needs to receive. Yes, in most cases we have moved beyond holding up a church budget and reminding our people of "the bills we have to pay." But the reality is that we often merely replaced the word *budget* with the word *mission*. What no one seemed to notice is that in both cases we are appealing to external motivation. As Smith and Emerson make clear in their book *Passing the Plate*, if American churches want to encourage more generous giving, we need to move away from a "pay the bills" culture and foster a "living the vision" culture in our churches.[6]

How do you foster a "living the vision" culture in our churches? We have to have identified a vision we are inviting our people to live! Then, too, we can't invite our sisters and brothers in Christ to live this vision unless we are first living it ourselves. As Gandhi's words remind us, "You must become what you want to create."

From time to time people will ask me, "You advocate this process. Does this process work every time?"

No. As I mentioned at the end of the previous chapter, I have experienced and witnessed successes and failures. Kotter admits that only one in four organizations that he worked with made significant change. My experience with churches is about the same. That may sound like bad news. Keep in mind, in Major League Baseball, anyone with a batting average of .250 or higher is considered a good hitter.

Then, too, the fact that a congregation may not succeed in its transformation process does not mean it was a waste of time. In a process that I led that failed, our team was able to look back and see our mistakes. We realized where more work had to be done. The failure was, in fact, a great learning process.

In the introduction, I listed five areas where the Ronsvalles indicated the church needed to focus its attention. The first one I listed was "Money is a difficult topic for the church to discuss." It is time to take a look at this.

CHAPTER SEVEN

The Power of Money

*The church has not appreciated the spiritual impact of money
on the believer, and so the church has immature believers.*[1]

—John Ronsvalle

As mentioned in the introduction, John and Sylvia Ronsvalle prepared their article "Giving Trends in the 1990s" in early 1990s. Within the next few years, several very significant stewardship-related books were published. The first of these was *God and Mammon in America* by Robert Wuthnow. Wuthnow sounded remarkably similar to Josiah Strong. Wuthnow argued that the church should be talking more about the power of money in the lives of its people. He acknowledged that many church leaders had learned to "mind their own business" when it came to issues of money.[2] He went on to state that one of his reasons for writing the book was to encourage religious leaders they could do something. He also acknowledged that he realized that religious leaders "seldom wanted to rock the boat, seldom wanted to offend their middle-class congregants, and certainly did not want to disrupt the flow of charitable giving on which their salaries depended."[3]

In these three observations—(1) the church should be talking about the power of money; (2) church leaders have learned to mind their own business; and (3) clergy do not want to rock the boat for fear of losing offering income—Wuthnow accurately summarized the church's predicament. He could have added a fourth. Most clergy, like their people, are also caught up in the American lifestyle. It is just as hard for them to hear and/or talk about the power of money.

Money, we are slowly beginning to rediscover, plays an immensely important role in people's lives. As I argued in chapter 4, I think the church made the unfortunate decision (probably not consciously but by default) that future money conversations would focus on the question, "How are we going to fund the church?" and not on "How are we going to talk about money?" This is the terminology that most churches adopted. The direction was set. We created the "pay the bills" mentality the Ronsvalles reported.

Indeed, for Christians, money actually has a two-fold impact. I am going to refer to the first one as the spiritual impact of money. To better understand this, we need to look at some biblical material.

In chapter 5, I clarified the difference between the world view of the steward, the *oikonomos*, and the nonsteward, the *autonomos*. The steward considers money and possessions as gifts from God to be managed according to God's intentions. The autonomous person considers money and possessions to be things that they own that can be used as they see fit. We now need to acknowledge that the biblical witness is that the autonomous approach to life is not without risk. In Deuteronomy 8:17–19, Moses warns the people of Israel: "Do not say to yourself, 'My power and the might of my own hand have gotten me this wealth... But remember the Lord your God... If you forget the Lord your God and follow other gods...you shall surely perish.'"

The biblical witness is clear. As soon as I begin to think and act as if "my power and the might of my own had have gotten me this wealth," i.e., autonomously, I have in fact begun to remove God from the equation. If I understand that what I have in my possession is there because I earned it, then I deny God's hand at work in the provision. The next step is to forget all that God has done in my life. The third step is to simply forget God. Notice that there is no open denial of God. God is simply forgotten.

Once one forgets God, declares the author of Deuteronomy, one will "follow other gods and worship them" (see Deut. 30:17, Joshua 24:15). This transition from worshipping God to forgetting God to necessarily "following other gods" is not one that most twenty-first-century American Christians readily understand. They think that if they chose to not worship God, the issue is settled. This is not the Old Testament witness.

Throughout the Gospels, Jesus repeatedly spoke about money and possessions and challenged his disciples and the crowds that followed him to be conscious of money and their relationship to it. Money is a very real threat to our relationship with God: "You cannot serve God and money" (Matthew 6:24).

I think it is very important to look more closely at what Jesus said. Jesus did not forbid serving two masters. He did not warn against serving two masters as if it were possible but, for some reason, not a good idea. He simply stated that it cannot be done. I deduce from this warning that Jesus anticipated that people would try to do this. It is my guess that there were people in Jesus's day that assumed they were doing a good job serving two. Jesus directly challenged this assumption.

It would seem that this assumption that we can serve two has not disappeared. In *God and Mammon in America*, Wuthnow observed that many Americans seem to be trying to do this very thing.[4]

St. Paul does not use the word *mammon* in any of his epistles. The word he uses in referring to our relationship to money is the Greek word *pleonexia*. It is often translated into English as *greed*. My favorite translation is "the insatiable desire for more." In Colossians 3:5, St. Paul refers to *pleonexia* as a form of idolatry.

Once again, in this word *idolatry*, we have another concept that is often misunderstood by the people in our churches. In my work with congregations, when people hear the word *idolatry*, the immediate connection most make is with Exodus 20:4: "You shall not make for yourself an idol." They typically think of Israel worshipping the golden calf (Exodus 32). They are then quick to point out that they have no idols in their churches.

It is at this point that I usually share the following quote from Luke T. Johnson's *Sharing Possessions: Mandate and Symbol of Faith:*

> Idolatry, in simple terms, is the choice of treating as ultimate and absolute that which is neither absolute or ultimate. We treat something as ultimate by the worship we pay it, meaning here, of course, neither the worship of lips or of incense but of service. Worship is service. Functionally, then, my god is that which I serve by my freedom. Whatever I claim as ultimate, the truth is that my god is that which rivets my attention, centers my activity, preoccupies my mind, and motivates my action. That in virtue of which I act is god; that for which I give up anything else is my god.[5]

Joshua's challenge to the people of Israel, "Choose this day who you will serve" (Joshua 24:15), is the same challenge we face today. The question is not whether we humans will put something at the center of our lives; we will. The question is "What will that thing be?"

G. K. Chesterton put it slightly differently: "When people stop believing in God, they do not believe in nothing; they believe in anything."

What are some of the things people believe in when they stop believing in God? Martin Luther identified a few of them: great learning, wisdom, power, prestige, family, and honor. Luther also thought they were clearly secondary. There was one thing more than any other that people tend to believe in when they don't believe in God.

> This I must explain a little more plainly, so that it may be understood and remembered, by citing some of the common examples of failure to observe this commandment. Many a person

thinks he has God and every-thing he needs when he has money and property; in them he trusts and of them he boasts so stubbornly and securely that he cares for no one. Surely such has a god—mammon by name, that is money and possessions—on which he fixes his whole heart. It is the most common idol on earth... This desire for wealth clings and cleaves to our nature all the way to the grave.[6]

What I have been attempting to describe is that the first part of dealing with the money issue is acknowledging that money can become an idol. An *idol* is "that in which I put my trust." Despite Jesus's warning, our temptation is to put some of our trust in God and some of our trust in money. Of course, we don't like to be reminded of this. We initially deny it is happening. When denial no longer works, we then get angry at the person reminding us of what we are doing. Is it any wonder most clergy avoid this topic?

In a previous chapter, I made a reference to Josiah Strong and Harvey Reeves Calkins. These were two of many voices that encouraged the church over a hundred years ago to stop focusing on funding. They sensed that the church needed to talk to its people about the power of mammon. Who did they think would lead this conversation? The clergy.

I mentioned earlier that in his book *God and Mammon in America*, Robert Wuthnow encouraged clergy to take the lead in helping the church address this very important issue. What Strong, Calkins, and Wuthnow failed to acknowledge is that while clergy may have some insight into mammon, they are no better prepared for the second part.

The second part is that money in and of itself is a highly emotionally charged topic. As I mentioned in chapter 3, the topic of money triggers reactivity. Almost everyone is uncomfortable talking about money. We need to examine our thoughts, feelings, and behaviors when to comes to money. With greater insight into our personal history with money, we may learn about where we acquired some of our present attitudes and, hopefully, respond more fully to God.

Over the years, I have come to learn that everyone has a money story. I was first introduced to this realm at a Clergy and Money Workshop in 1988. It was sponsored by the Alban Institute and The Ministry of Money.[7] I was not at all sure what we were going to cover. I got my first clue when I received my preworkshop homework in a mailing. I was sent materials to help me write my money autobiography. Elizabeth O'Conner, in her book *Letters to Scattered Pilgrims*,[8], describes an assignment she gave to one of her classes. The class was told to (1) read Luke and (2) write a three-page autobiography which deals with the meaning of money in your life.

The instructions we were given was to identify events in our lives where money played an important role. We were given a list of questions to consider but were encouraged to write down whatever came to mind. A key factor was making sure we put the experience or event in writing. We could not just think about it. We had to put it on paper. We were also told that we would *not* be giving this writing assignment to anyone else to read. It was just for ourselves. We were encouraged to be as honest and forthright as possible.

The clergy attending the workshop came from a wide variety of denominations and from all across the United States. None of us had met before. We spent the first evening just getting to know each other a little better. Over the course of the weekend, our group covered a wide range of topics. There was a session on the financial binds unique to clergy, i.e., living in a rectory/parsonage. Because we live in a society where money is often equated with value, we talked about clergy salaries. All in all, it was an excellent workshop.

By far the most moving portion of the event was when we were given the opportunity to share some of incidents from our money autobiographies. It was amazing how each person's story was different, and yet we could all see the similarities. I found that listening to the stories of others triggered all kinds of money memories for me. I found myself making notes on additional stories I wanted to add to my money autobiography when I got home.

During the closing session, one of the leaders observed that during this workshop, we had violated one of the last taboos of our society; we had talked openly and personally about money. He also acknowledged that we had simply begun our journeys with money. There was much more to learn if we were willing to keep looking and learning.

One of the most helpful resources I found in this area was a book by Olivia Mellan entitled *Money Harmony*.[9] The book is very helpful in identifying some money myths. Money myths are global beliefs about all the wonderful, almost magical things that money can do for us. These myths include money = happiness, money = love, money = power, money = freedom, money = self-worth, money = security, and money = self-sufficiency.[10]

Another amazing book in this area is Jacob Needleman's *Money and the Meaning of Life*.[11] The book came as a result of an undergraduate course of the same name that Needleman taught at San Francisco State University. As the story goes, the course became so popular that he could not accommodate all the students who wanted to take it. He was asked to put his material in a book so it could be shared with more people. Here is a taste: "A superficial understanding of the place of money in a spiritual life is no longer much help. Without a long work on oneself, it is impossible in contemporary conditions to be generous and free in regard to money… It means finding the precise place of money at the heart of the most important undertaking in our lives—the search to become what we are meant to be."[12]

In the meantime, I had been doing a lot of thinking and talking with colleagues about the important learnings that we all derived from writing our own money autobiographies. I thought it was a resource that we could and should share with the rest of the church. I had been preparing and leading stewardship workshops for years. I decided to incorporate the money autobiography into one of them.

The event "Walking in Newness of Life" was designed to be a weekend event; Friday night through Sunday afternoon. Congregations were asked to send a team to the event. This team was to include the pastor and at least four other persons. Our desire was to help congregations begin building the team they would need to lead stewardship renewal in their church.

In preparation for the event, we asked each participant to write a money autobiography. Our plan was to have each congregational team spend ninety minutes on Saturday afternoon sharing from their money autos. We assumed that the clergy would lead this process.

What we discovered was that the clergy were not ready to do this.[13] They were just as new to this experience as their people were. I was one of four leaders of the event. All four of us had done a fair amount of reflecting on our money autos. These pastors had not. As the four of us walked around visiting the various groups, we observed that all of the groups were struggling with this exercise.

When the leadership team gathered to review the event, we all acknowledged that money autobiography session did not work well. For some reasons, we thought the pastors could just jump in. That was totally unfair. We had succumbed to the quick-fix mentality. We learned again that when it comes to the emotional power of money, nothing will be quick or easy.

Over the last twenty-plus years, there have been other voices that have said that the church needs to help its people look at the spiritual and emotional power of money. In each case, the assumption is that clergy must play a key role. Robert Wuthnow went so far as to state, "Clergy need to be challenged to do a better job".[14]

I agree that clergy need to play a key role. I also know that it will not help to challenge clergy if, at the same time, you do not offer the help they will need. As I have been saying all along, money issues are very emotionally charged. This is not easy stuff. Growth usually implies change. Change usually involves pain. Most of us try to avoid pain.

Several years ago, I developed a program called Journey into Freedom. It is designed to help clergy better understand the emotional power of money in their own lives. Obviously, this is not something clergy can be compelled to do. It has to be something they want to do. Over the years, I have had the privilege of walking with many others on their money journeys. Discovering the meaning, the power, and the pain of one's relationship to money—especially in a culture so centered around it—is a fierce spiritual struggle.

For people who want to begin exploring the power of money in their own lives, I heartily recommend Rosemary Williams's *A Woman's Book of Money and Spiritual Vision: Putting Your Financial Values into Financial Practice.*[15] First of all, it is not just for women; it works for men equally well. It is very much a workbook. You will be encouraged to write a money autobiography. There is nothing magical to the book. The more effort you put into thoughtfully answering the questions provided, the more insight you will gain.

When it comes to the emotional and spiritual power of money I want to include two caveats:

1. There is no quick fix. Discovering the power of money in my life continues for me to be a lifelong process. I wrote my first money autobiography in 1988. Thirty years later, I am still working on it.

2. This exploration is best done with others. It is too easy for us to fool ourselves and live in denial. It is too easy to say, "That is not my problem."

"Central to my theme is the conviction that we cannot make a serious religious quest without coming to terms with our burden of possessions and wealth" (Donald Hinze).[16]

"In a society flooded with affluence, biblical ethics are too often lost in the din. Church members left to themselves will unthinkingly adapt to Mammon's agenda unless provided with an active alternative" (John Ronsvalle).[17]

In one of our many conversations in the mid-1990s, Bob Lynn mused: "One of our great opportunities – indeed privileges – during the coming turn-of-the-century era is to help Christians face up to this crisis about the meaning of money. You can lead the way. A new conversation about the mystery of the Christian idea of money is coming over the horizon of the future."[18]

CHAPTER EIGHT

A New Narrative

The kingdom [of God] is not a geographical place; rather it is a relationship of power, in which God and creature are properly aligned.

—Luke T. Johnson[1]

I was part of a two-year confirmation program in my home congregation when I was in seventh and eighth grade. The second year was taught by our senior pastor, Pastor Ludwig. On the first day of class, Pastor Ludwig explained to our class that for the next eight months, we were going to be looking at the two most important questions in life: (1) Is there a god? And if so, what is god like? (2) How must I live this life to put the most into it and get the most out of it? I do not remember too much of what we talked about that year, but I have never forgotten those questions.

I noted in chapter 4 that the conversion of Constantine in 312 C.E. was an incredible turning point in the life of the church. Christianity was no longer persecuted. It was now the preferred religion of the empire. The distinctive lifestyle it espoused was soon lost amid the rapid influx of new members. I noted that the funding of the church by the Roman Empire had a dramatic impact on people's giving. Within the next one hundred years, the church faced another turning point. In this case the choice was theological, but the ramifications were no less profound.

St. Augustine was born November 13, 354 C.E., in present-day Algeria. He served as bishop of Hippo from 396 to 430 C.E. He is referred to as one of the Latin Fathers of the Church and perhaps the most significant Christian thinker after St. Paul. Augustine created a theological system. At center of this system was his concept of original sin. Original sin was the sin of disobedience depicted in the Adam and Eve story in Genesis 3:1–24.

With Augustine's thinking in mind, if we look at Pastor Ludwig's first question, the answer we come up with is yes, there is a God. However, sin entered the world through the disobedience of Adam and Eve. God's perfect world had been destroyed; human life had fallen into sin. God was not so much the source of life and love as a likely source of judgment.

This way of thinking was reinforced in my life every Sunday morning when I sat in church. My weekly worship experience included a confession of sins. Every Sunday morning for the first eighteen years of my life, along with the others gathered for worship, I said, "Almighty God, our maker and Redeemer, we poor sinners confess unto thee, that we are by nature sinful and unclean, and that we have sinned against Thee by thought, word and deed. Wherefore we flee for refuge to Thine infinite mercy, seeking and imploring Thy grace, for the sake of our Lord Jesus Christ."[2]

Every Sunday, I was reminded that I was a sinner for whom a price had to be paid. Jesus's death on the cross was the price that God demanded. How was I to live my life? I needed to acknowledge that I was a sinner. If I kept confessing my sins every Sunday, God, because of Jesus, would "wipe my slate clean" for another week. However, this forgiveness was seemingly only good for a week. I would need to return the next Sunday and repeat the process. When our liturgy included a service of Holy Communion, I was reminded that Jesus's blood was "shed for you, and for many, for the remission of sins." It was made abundantly clear to me that sin was the issue.

It so happened that in precisely the same year, 354 C.E., another future Roman Catholic theologian was born. His name was Pelagius. He would later become a British monk. He did not have as pessimistic view of humankind as Augustine did. Pelagius trusted original blessing more than original sin and focused on the individual's ability, through grace, to grow into Christ.

As our history tells us, the church of Pelagius's day decried his insights and defended Augustine's doctrine of original sin. Some claimed that Pelagius denied the importance of grace. It seems to me he was just emphasizing orthopraxy.[3] As I have learned from reading a lot of Fr. Richard Rohr, Franciscanism, insofar as it actually imitated Francis of Assisi, emphasized an alternative orthodoxy. This different view on what really matters had much more to do with how one lived as opposed to mere belief systems (i.e., believing the right words). In one of his letters, Pelagius wrote, "You will realize that doctrines are inventions of the human mind, as it tried to penetrate the mystery of God. You will realize that Scripture itself is the work of human minds, recording the example and teaching of Jesus. Thus, it is not what you believe that matters; it is how you respond with your heart and your actions. It is not believing in Christ that matters; it is becoming like him."[4]

My purpose in mentioning Pelagius is to remind us that the church had an alternative to the atonement theology that Augustine championed. Is it too late to look again at this alternative vision?

The theology of Augustine emphasizes the split and the unbridgeable distance between creator and creation, between God and the human. In spite of the ecological unity of all creation that modern man has come to understand, to this day, much of Christianity keeps emphasizing a problem (original sin) instead of beginning with the wonderful unity between creation and creator (original blessing).

In my work with congregations, I often mention this difference between original sin and original blessing. To this day, in almost every case, people are familiar with the idea of original sin. They are not so sure about original blessing. And so, I typically take them back to Genesis, chapter 1: "So God created humankind in his image; in the image of God he created them; male and female he created them. God blessed them and said, 'Be fruitful and multiply, and fill the earth and subdue it; and have dominion...over everything that moves upon the earth... God saw everything he had made, and indeed, it was very good'" (Gen. 1:27–28,31).

Genesis 1 is very clear. It begins with the God the creator. The human is obviously the creature. This original blessing story tells us that God provided everything the human needed to thrive. The human was even given dominion (Genesis 1:26) but not ownership.[5] The human was put in charge not to dominate but to tend and help to flourish. The key was that the human needed to keep in mind that he was in a working relationship with the creator God. He had a God-given responsibility to care for creation.

In his commentary on Genesis,[6] Walter Brueggemann noted that this relation was "grounded in a mystery of faithful commitment." He then continued,

> "This affirmation requires the abandonment of two false assumptions that are alive in the church. First, the relation of creator and creation is often understood in terms of coercion and necessity because of the power of mechanistic models of reality and tyrannical notions of God. But the relation of creator and creation-creature in Genesis 1:1–2:4 is not one of coercion. It is rather one of free, gracious commitment and invitation. The linkage is one of full trust rather than requirement or obligation. Second, there is a common inclination to confine the matter of God's grace to individual, guilt-related issues of morality. But the text affirms graciousness on the part of God as his transforming disposition towards the whole world."[7]

Obviously, I agree with Brueggemann; there are two false assumptions alive in the church. My interest is not in trying to prove the church made a poor choice 1,600 years ago. Rather, I am hoping that the church is prepared to make a new and more hopeful choice today.

I think the difference between these two visions, original sin and original blessing, is seen even more dramatic if we look again at Jesus's announcement in Mark 1:15.

I grew up in a church heavily influenced by St. Augustine's theology. I knew I was sinful and unclean. To hear Jesus say, "The time is fulfilled" did sound promising, possibly even exciting. However, these words were followed by "the kingdom of God is at hand" (King James Version). Since I knew that I was a sinner, the announcement of the arrival of God's kingdom was not necessarily good news. It meant that God was coming to judge the world. Luckily, I was also given some good advice: "Repent and believe the good news." *Repent* I thought meant to say I was sorry for my sins, and *believe* meant to trust that Jesus died for me, and for his sake, I would be forgiven and experience God's salvation.

Since I now think in terms of *original blessing*, I hear Jesus announcement very differently. "Time's up!"[8] God had been very patient with humankind for a long time, hoping we might get it right. God chose the Jews to be the bearer of his word, his plan, his intention. They got some of it right. They were right that the God of Gods was not some local deity. They were right in thinking they were a chosen people. They got it wrong if they thought that, in choosing them, God was excluding others. They were chosen to carry the message that God loved all of creation.

"Time's up" means that God is moving away from that old plan and instituting a new plan. The initial announcement of this new plan is that "God's Kingdom is here and now." It did not involve driving the Roman army out of Palestine. This kingdom was not something we'd experience only after we die. God sent Jesus to announce and clarify this new plan. The key was to first listen to what Jesus had to say. If you listened to Jesus and watched him for any time at all, you would realize that he was challenging you to open your mind to a new reality (i.e., repent). But then, he was not only inviting you to see things differently but also to change the way you lived based on this new reality. Or as Pelagius said it, "Become like Jesus."

"The Kingdom of God [for Jesus] was never about words and ideas, aphorisms and parables, sayings and dialogues. It was about a way of life" (John Dominic Crossan).[9]

Again, Pastor Ludwig's first question was, "Is there god? If so, what is god like?" The answer we receive in Genesis 1 is that there is indeed a god, a loving and attentive creator. This creator wants the very best for all of creation. This God wants the human to play a role in helping this creation to flourish as God intended.

God, the owner, has a plan for creation. I am called to be a steward. The focus is no longer on our individual private perfection—or what Thomas Merton called our personal salvation project—but rather, we become fully human and useable by opening our hearts to God. A steward's job description is to "help carry out God's plan." Before I can carry out God's plan, I need to know God's plan. I need to read the instructions. I need to immerse myself in God's word. If I do, I will discover that I am a child of God. I will discover that God is relational, and not propositional. After all, the Lord's prayer begins with "Our father."

But even this can be a problem. Some people do not want a relationship; they want religion. I believe that the God of love is looking for relationship, but I also realize that love is demanding and expectant. Love also offer joys and passion. It might be easier to simply go to church.

Pastor Ludwig's second question was, "How shall I live this life to put the most into it and get the most out of it?" The answer Genesis 1 gives us is (1) by remembering that there is a God and (2) by remembering, therefore, that I am a steward and not an owner.

This is the incredible responsibility given to the humankind; that by our actions, we humans will reflect God's will, plan, and loving desire for creation. The way I can put the most into my life and get the most out of it is by living my life as a faithful *eikon*. As Jesus said so plainly in John 10:10, "I came that they may have life, and have it abundantly."

So why don't more humans listen to this amazing announcement of what God is inviting us to be? Part of the problem is we humans tend to prefer heavenly transactions to our own transformation.

Another part of the problem is that, as silly as it may sound, we simply forget. You will recall that in chapter 5 I mentioned the observation of Dr. Walter Brueggemann. He suggested that the central theme of the Old Testament was not "man, the sinner" but "Will we remember or will we forget?" Remember and live; forget and die.

This thought is echoed by John Shea. "Some spiritual traditions say that the enemy we struggle against is sin. There are other traditions that say the real enemy is forgetfulness. The inability to remember who you are—your identity—you forget you are on a mission."[10]

Why are we so prone to forgetting? I think huge part of our conundrum is our affluence. "The problem with affluence, then, is not that there is anything wrong with prosperity itself but that material abundance often leads to spiritual amnesia."[11]

CHAPTER NINE

A Transforming Church

God loves us as we are, but much too much to leave us there.

—William Sloan Coffin[1]

Back in the mid-1970s, while I was serving in my first parish, a colleague asked me to accompany him to a program in Philadelphia. He said the program had something to do with the church and business. The presenter was going to be a business consultant by the name of Peter Drucker. I was not familiar with Drucker's work, so I did a little research before the event. I discovered he was a very interesting man. He was a leader in the development of management education. He was credited with inventing the concept known as management by objective. I assumed that part of his presentation was going to include something like "the church needs to be run in a more businesslike manner."

I don't recall much of what Drucker said that day, but I have never forgotten his observation that "The church is not like a business. In business your goal is to satisfy the customer. The church has one essential product: a changed human being."

I confess what when I first heard these words, my initial response was, "Who does this guy think he is that he can tell me, a pastor of the church, what the church is about?"

I'm pretty sure I stopped listening to Drucker at that point. I think I spent the rest of the morning going over in my head how I had been trained to be a loving, caring, and compassionate shepherd. It was my job to tend (Jesus's) sheep and remind my people every Sunday that they are loved and forgiven. No professor in the seminary I attended ever said anything remotely like "The church has one essential product: a changed human being."

It took a while for my initial knee-jerk reaction to Drucker's observation to cool down. I recall sitting down a few days later with my senior pastor and talking about what Drucker had said. Pastor Dave acknowledged that most pastors he knew graduated from seminary thinking it was their call to care for and nurture the flock, not transform it. He also acknowledged that most pastors are careful about what they say and do for fear of rocking the boat, getting their people upset or anxious.[2] Pastor Dave then quoted another consultant, "We can't become what God wants us to be by staying the way we are."[3]

Richard Hudnut-Beumler[4] addressed this idea of change in a congregation by suggesting that pastors and congregations really need to figure out if their congregation is going to be a bartender or a therapist to its members. As we know, a bartender can play the role of confessor and listen attentively to the cares and concerns of the people he is serving. However, in the end, all he can offer is a drink and a ready ear. A therapist, on the other hand, is oriented to not only listening to those cares and insecurities but also helping the client do something about them.

Is the goal of the church "a changed human being"? How do we see the church? As bartender or therapist?

One of the authors that I began reading when I began consulting with congregations was Lyle Schaller. It is my sense that Lyle was widely considered by pastors to be the most important and influential observer of church culture during the twentieth century in the United States. In his 1993 book, *Strategies for Change*,[5] Lyle gave us a slightly different dichotomy. He argued that the critical factor we need to keep in mind is "the vast difference between high commitment covenant communities and voluntary associations."[6] Schaller was not optimistic about the future of the church as a voluntary organization.

There were others who were less subtle. "The church is not supposed to be a place where everybody gets their needs met. It is supposed to be a place where we are transformed by God's grace into something we are not."[7]

I would put St. Paul in this less-subtle group. In the fourth chapter of Ephesians, Paul writes to the Christians in Ephesus about "living a life worthy of their calling." He goes on to describe the different kinds of leaders God gives to the church. He then describes what pastors and teachers were to be about: "To equip the saints for the work of ministry, for building up the body of Christ, until all of us come to the unity faith…to maturity, to the measure of the full stature of Christ" (Ephesians 4:11–13).

Paul was never reluctant to acknowledge that the people in the Christian communities he visited were at many different stages in their faith journeys. Some were more mature than others. He was also not afraid to say, "We all must grow up" (Ephesians 4:15). We all have further growing to do. God is still working in us and on us to grow in Christ, to make His mind, His way of doing things, His norms, and His way of operating become our way of thinking and living.

In the final paragraph of "Giving Trends," the Ronsvalles began to summarize their observations. They suggested that if we do not address the necessary changes we need to make in stewardship attitudes, at least two things will happen. First, things will get tight financially. Congregations, dioceses, and denominations will receive fewer and fewer funds and will, therefore, be unable to carry out its work to meet domestic and global need. As congregational income decreases, budgets get adjusted. The cost to maintain a building is not decreasing. Congregations will need to keep more and more of their offerings at home to pay the bills. Less and less will be given away. We already see this happening.

The second issue is that if the church does not "combine greater economic substance with our declaration of faith, the church risks being marginalized in North American Society." This too is already happening. Recall that in chapter 4, I described the phenomenal growth of the church during the first three centuries. This growth was not explainable by superior theology. It was the distinctive and compelling way Christians lived. So how are we doing?

In their 2008 book, *Passing the Plate: Why American Christians Don't Give away More Money*, the authors, Christian Smith and Michael O. Emerson, wrote about what was happening to giving within the church. The authors of this book are not theologians but sociologists. They did not comment on whether Christians should be more generous. Their focus was on why they seem to not be. In essence, their observation was that American Christians behave exactly like all other Americans do. On the whole, there is nothing distinctive in how they live and certainly not in their giving.

About the same time that a friend recommended that I read *Passing the Plate*, another colleague recommended *The Didache* by Aaron Milavec. I vaguely remembered hearing about this ancient text when I was in seminary. It was fascinating to be reminded that this document captured an early moment[8] in the formation of Christianity. The text was not a theological work. It does not even mention Jesus. It describes how the people in this community were going to live together. This was *the* critical question. The opening words are "There are two ways [of living]: one of life and one of death. And there is a great difference between the two ways." The Jesus movement associated with the *Didache* set about to form and transform the lives of those who wanted to be a part of their community.

In the midst of describing this very early Christian community, Milavec made the following observation: "Any community that cannot artfully and effectively pass on its cherished way of life as a program for graced existence cannot long endure. Any way of life that cannot be clearly specified, exhibited, and differentiated from the alternative modes operative within the surrounding culture is doomed to growing insignificance and to gradual assimilation."[9]

The Ronsvalles warned that the church could be marginalized. Milavec wrote that without a cherished way of life, a community is doomed to "growing insignificance and gradual assimilation." It seems clear to me that this is what is happening to many of our churches.

In Romans 12:2, Paul wrote, "Do not be conformed to this world, but be transformed by the renewing of your minds." When I mention this verse to congregations that I meet with, I usually follow up with a question: "What is your congregation doing to transform the lives of your people?" The answers vary, but they usually refer to the something that the congregation has been doing for the last twenty-five years. When I suggest to pastors that their people may be unwittingly conforming to the powerful culture that surrounds them, I am usually told, "Oh no. They are just very busy."

Really? Busy?

There seems be a total denial of what is happening within their own community. There is an old saying: "If it ain't broke, don't fix it." I keep encountering church people who think nothing is broken. Therefore, they don't think they need to fix (change) anything.

What does the future hold for Christians? Truly transformed people change the world while fundamentally unchanged people soon conform to the world. Culture will win out every time if it is not also critiqued. I know that I am echoing the advice of many when I suggest that we Christians have to disestablish ourselves. We need to be able to distinguish between a life in Christ and the American way of life.

In 1990, Douglas John Hall wrote, "The only adequate response to the great physical and spiritual problems of our historical moment is for the human inhabitants of this planet to acquire, somehow, a new way of imagining themselves."[10]

In 2008, Smith and Emerson advised the church that it needed to move away from the "pay the bills" mentality it has instilled in its members. They suggested that the church needed to move in the direction of helping its people live the vision of what they say God calls them to be.[11]

In 2012, Diana Butler Bass wrote, "What will make a difference to the future is awakening to a faith that fully communicates God's love—a love that transforms how we believe, what we do, and who we are in the world."[12]

What is the new way of "imagining ourselves"? What is this vision we should be inviting our people to live? What is this "awakening to faith that will transform how we believe, what we do and how we live in the world"? The people of God need to be invited to understand themselves and live their lives as stewards. As Mark Allen Powell said so clearly, "Biblically speaking, stewardship is our mission, not just a means of funding our mission."[13]

I continue to work with congregations. I am usually invited to meet with some of the congregation's leaders to talk about the future of their congregation. They hope I can offer them a plan to save their congregation, i.e., receive the income they need. They are typically surprised when I tell them that stewardship is *not* about funding the mission; it is the mission. We were called by Jesus to make disciples. A disciple is a person who is learning about God's intention for all of life. A steward is a disciple who takes what they have learned and puts it into practice. As I say to people all of the time, "If you don't live it, you don't believe it."

From time to time, people have asked me, "So you don't care about the church?"

My response is always, "Sure I do. But the first thing Jesus told the eleven to do was to make disciples, not to start a church." History suggests that Jesus's followers quickly realized that it is very hard to be faithful alone. They needed a community of believers to support and challenge them.

Here is the question we need to answer: "Is the church ready to become a covenant community that offers a way of life that can be clearly specified, exhibited, and differentiated from the alternative modes operative within the surrounding culture?" If we are not constantly working on our own transformation, we will, most likely, conform to the culture around us. We will be assimilated.

One of the problems we need to acknowledge is that the idea of faith being life changing is foreign to many of our people. Having said that, I hope it does not sound like we need to threaten God's people. I think we need talk this way because we want to invite people to discover the joy-filled and meaningful life God intends. Stewardship is not about what God wants *from* you, but what God wants *for* you.

"We must begin with this basic vision: our goal is to find the life that God wants us to have, in the confidence that this will be the best life we could possibly have."[14]

The powerful thing about what happened in Mt. Holly and then in Turnersville was not so much the better cash flow. It was the fact that people really invested themselves in the idea of being a steward. It gave them an identity. It was not a creedal statement of who they thought Jesus was. But rather, it answered the question, "How is God calling me to live everyday of my life?"

"We need to move beyond seeing stewardship as a matter of techniques and programs. It is a lifestyle and journey into the very heart of God."[15]

"The church is not engaged in marketing to build itself up. It is a training and teaching body of Christ. Our deeds will be our message. Christians will live differently in a compelling way."[16] People outside the church are looking for authentic community. We have something to offer.

"A church is a place where we try to think, speak, and act in God's way and not in the way of a fear-filled world. A church is a home for brothers and sisters to dwell in unity, to rest and be healed, and to let go of their defenses and be free - free from worries, free from tensions, free to laugh, free to cry. A place to live *as if God reigned* [emphasis mine] here and now."[17]

The church has everything the world is looking for, we just don't know we've got it!

APPENDIX

What Is Going on in Stewardship?[1]

John and Sylvia Ronsvalle, president and executive president of *empty tomb, inc.*, wrote an essay for the 1990 *North American Conference on Christian Philanthropy Report* entitled "Giving Trends and Their Implications."[2] What follows are some excerpts from their conclusions:

1. Money is a difficult topic for the church to discuss.
2. Perhaps as a result, crisis fundraising has become standard practice. As one pastor noted, "The wolf at the door is actually welcome, since it provides a clear opportunity to go to the congregation and express the need for money in an acceptable way."
3. Pastors feel ill-prepared for the stewardship task with little or no training in seminary even though fundraising is one of the major activities in actual practice.
4. Money can be used as a tool to exert control, sometimes over the pastor directly; it can be used by an individual to assert his or her value.

[1.] North American Conference on Christian Philanthropy 1990, Ecumenical Center for Stewardship Studies.

[2.] John and Sylvia Ronsvalle, "Giving Trends and Their Implications for the 1990s," 143–148.

5. The typical congregational member's approach to the budget might be summarized by a "wait and see" attitude. There is a concern to not give the church more money that is needed. Budgets are not funded until the end of the year and then frequently not fully funded.

6. One pastor characterized giving patterns as a "pay the bill" mentality. Talking about a denominational program in Asia, he said, "If the church in India sent us a bill, we'd pay it."

7. A lay person summarized this perception in a slightly different way. Congregation members have become purchasers of services (youth programs, a nice building to have ceremonies) rather than stewards returning a portion of what they have to God.

8. The general feeling was that attitudes toward money and stewardship require deep changes but that those changes will not come about easily or quickly.

One might borrow from secular culture to find descriptive labels. In an article talking about the role of the pastor in the congregation, one pastor labeled certain patterns of pastoral behavior within a congregation a dependency model of ministry. Building on this application of secular psychological term to describe dynamics within a congregation, perhaps one might consider stewardship in terms of dysfunctional patterns.

From a psychological viewpoint, one might term *dysfunctional* as the inability to act on one's desires in appropriate ways because of established patterns of counterproductive behavior. Certainly, in some ways, congregations cannot be termed *dysfunctional* as most congregations can mount a building campaign, for example, even as they do not meet their monthly bills.

In summary, it should be recognized that a great portion of the general population, and thus many church members, are richer than before. In spite of this increased income, giving as a percent of income has exhibited a definite downward trend over a period of years, a trend that may now be escalating.

At the congregational level, stewardship is perceived as a difficult topic to undertake both because money in general is difficult to discuss and because people have changed from stewards to consumers. The increased affluence and changes in society may have either caused or reinforced negative patterns in congregations that need to be addressed before necessary changes in stewardship will come about. To not address this need for change in stewardship attitudes is to limit the church's ability to live up to its giving potential and thus its potential for meeting domestic and global need. If the church does not combine greater economic substance with its declaration of faith, the church risks being marginalized in North American society.

NOTES

Introduction

1. T. A. Kantonen, *A Theology of Christian Stewardship* (Philadelphia: Muhlenburg Press, 1956), vii.

2. G. K. Chesterton, *What's Wrong with the World* (Dover Publications, 2007; first published 1920).

3. Ecumenical Center for Stewardship Studies, *North American Conference on Christian Philanthropy* (printed report, 1990).

4. See "Appendix."

5. John and Sylvia Ronsvalle, "Giving Trends and Their Implications for the 1990s," in *North American Conference on Christian Philanthropy* (printed report, 1990).

Chapter One

1. Charles R. Lane, *Ask, Thank, Tell* (Minneapolis: Augsburg-Fortress, 2006).
    Chapter 5 has a lot to say about the role of the clergy in the stewardship process.

2. Lynn Twist, "Chapter 3 – Scarcity: The Great Lie," in *The Soul of Money* (New York: W.W. Norton & Co., 2003).

3. Wallace Fisher, *All the Good Gifts: On Doing Biblical Stewardship* (Minneapolis: Augsburg Publishing House, 1979), 71.

4. I'll address this issue in greater depth in chapter 3.

5. Edwin H. Friedman, *Generation to Generation: Family Process in Church and Synagogue* (New York: The Guilford Press, 1985), 27.

Chapter Two

1. Peter L. Steinke, *A Door Set Open*, (Herndon, VA: The Alban Institute, 2010), 27.

2. _____, *The Clergy Journal* (Inner Grove Heights, MN: Logos Publications).

3. Commission for Financial Support of the Evangelical Lutheran Church in America, *A Congregational Planning Option* (Chicago, 1989), 25–26.

4. Robert Wuthnow, "Pious Materialism: How Americans View Faith and Money," in *Christian Century* (March 3, 1993), 238–242.

5. Robert Wuthnow, *God and Mammon in America* (New York: The Free Press, 1994).

Chapter Three

1. William Sloan Coffin, *Credo* (Louisville, KY: Westminster John Knox Press, 2004), 125.

2. Peter L. Steinke, *Healthy Congregations: A Systems Approach* (Herndon, VA: Alban Institute, 1993).

3. Peter L. Steinke, "Chapter Two: Anxiety and Reactivity," in *How Your Church Family Works*, (Herndon, VA: Alban Institute, 2006).

4. This program was started by Edwin Friedman and is run out of the Center for Family Process in Bethesda, MD.

5. Edwin H. Friedman, *A Failure of Nerve: Leadership in the Age of the Quick Fix* (New York: Seabury Books, 2007).

6. Steven R. Covey, *Principle-Centered Leadership* (New York: Simon & Schuster, 1990).

7. Ibid., 17.

8. Murray Bowen, MD, was a clinical professor at Georgetown University Medical Center. He was one of the founders of family therapy and the originator of family systems theory.

9. John Shea, *Following Jesus* (Maryknoll, NY: Orbis Books, 2010), 111.

Chapter Four

1. See Aaron Milavec, *The Didache: Faith, Hope, & Life of the Earliest Christian Communities, 50–70 C.E.* (Mahwah, NJ: The Newman Press, 2003).

2. Rodney Stark, *The Rise of Christianity* (San Francisco: Harper Collins, 1997).

3. In fact, some of the early colonies, e.g., Massachusetts, supported the church through taxes.

4. Josiah Strong, *Our Country: Its Possible Future and Its Present Crisis* (New York: Bible House for the American Home Mission Society, 1885).

5. Harvey Reeves Calkins, *A Man and His Money* (New York: The Methodist Book Concern, 1920).

6. Kantonen, *A Theology of Christian Stewardship.*

7. Ronsvalle, "Giving Trends," 148.

8. Douglas John Hall, *The Steward: A Biblical Symbol Come of Age* (Friendship Press). Reprinted by William B. Eerdmans, Grand Rapids, MI, 1990.

9. Peter M. Senge, *The Fifth Discipline: The Art and Practice of the Learning Organization* (New York: Crown Business, 2006), 61.

10. Hall, *The Steward,* 16.

11. Dean R. Hoge and Douglas Griffin, *Research On Factors Influencing Giving to Religious Bodies* (Indianapolis, IN: Ecumenical Center for Stewardship Studies, 1992).

12. John and Sylvia Ronsvalle, *Behind The Stained Glass Window: Money Dynamics in the Church* (Grand Rapids, MI: Baker Books, 1996).

13. Loren B. Mead, *Financial Meltdown in the Mainline?* (Alban Institute Publication, 1998.

14. William Avery, "Avoiding the Connection between Faith and Money," in *Faith in Action* (1996), 9–13.

15. Martin Marty, *Giving Magazine* (Ecumenical Stewardship Center) vo. 1 (1999).

16. Robert Wuthnow, *The Crisis in the Churches: Spiritual Malaise, Fiscal Woe* (New York: Oxford University Press, 1997).

17. Christian Smith and Michael O. Emerson, *Passing the Plate: Why Christians Don't Give Away More Money* (New York: Oxford University Press, 2008).

18. Ibid., 180.

Chapter Five

1. T. A. Kantonen, "The Motivation of Christian Stewardship," in *Select Stewardship Sermons* (Lima, Ohio: The C.S.S. Publishing Co., 1973), 52–53.

2. Calkins, *A Man and His Money*, 59.

3. John Reumann, *Stewardship & the Economy of God* (Grand Rapids, MI: William B. Eerdmans Publishing, 1992), 12–13.

4. John C Haughey, S.J., *Virtue and Affluence: The Challenge of Wealth* (Kansas City, MO: Sheed & Ward, 1997), 73.

5. Luke T. Johnson, *Sharing Possessions: Mandate and Symbol of Faith* (Philadelphia: Fortress Press, 1981), 100.

6. Mark Allan Powell, *Giving to God* (Grand Rapids, MI: William B. Eerdmmans Publishing, 2006), 87.

7. At the time, Brueggemann was serving as the William Marcellus McPheeter's professor of Old Testament at Columbia Theological Seminary, Decatur, GA.

8. Mark 1:15; Eugene Peterson, *The Message* (Colorado Springs, CO: Navpress Publishing Group, 2003), 76.

9. The NRSV translates the Greek word *teleios* as "perfect." I prefer the English word *mature*. St. Paul summarized his entire ministry in Colossians 1:28b: "So that we may present everyone mature in Christ."

10. Smith and Emerson, *Passing the Plate*, 180.

11. Hall, *The Steward*, 16–17.

12. John P. Kotter, "Leading Change: Why Transformation Efforts Fail," *Harvard Business Review*, March–April 1995, 59–67.

Chapter Six

1. *How to Improve Financial Stewardship* (Evangelical Lutheran Church in America, 1996) outlines the various response methods. It also includes the strengths and weaknesses of each method.

2. Martin Marty, *Giving Magazine* (Ecumenical Stewardship Center) vo. 1 (1999).

3. Covey, *Principle-Centered Leadership*, 17.

4. In chapter 2, I mentioned the fundraiser where we did this calculation to determine our present level of giving.

5. Powell, *Giving to God*, 19.

6. See chapter 4, "extrinsic vs. intrinsic."

Chapter Seven

1. John and Sylvia Ronsvalle, *Behind The Stained Glass Windows*, 141.

2. Robert Wuthnow, *God and Mammon*, 4.

3. Ibid. p. 10.

4. Ibid., see chapter 1 "Serving Two Masters."

5. Johnson, *Sharing Possessions*, 49.

6. Theodore G. Tappert, ed., *The Book of Concord* (Philadelphia: Fortress Press, 1959), 356–366.

7. This ministry, started in 1971, was the idea of Don McClanen in cooperation with the Church of the Savior in Washington, D.C.

8. Elizabeth O'Conner, *Letters to Scattered Pilgrims* (New York: Harper & Row, 1982), 228–30.

9. Olivia Mellan, *Money Harmony* (New York: Walker and Co., 1994).

10. Ibid., 50 ff.

11. Jacob Needleman, *Money and the Meaning of Life* (New York: Doubleday, 1994).

12. Ibid., 15–16.

13. Steinke echoes this in *A Door Set Open*, p. 57.

14. Wuthnow, *The Crisis in the Churches*, 7.

15. Rosemary Williams, *A Woman's Book of Money and Spiritual Vision* (Philadelphia: Innis Free Press, 2001).

16. Donald Hinze, *To Give and Give Again: A Christian Imperative for Generosity* (New York: Pilgrim Press, 1990). Xi.

17. John and Sylvia Ronsvalle, *The State of Church Giving through 2016* (Champaign, Illinois: empty tomb, inc., 2018), 139.

18. Robert Wood Lynn, Bangor Theological Seminary

Chapter Eight

1. Luke T. Johnson, *The Creed*, (New York: Doubleday, 2003), 208.

2. _____, *The Common Service Book of the Lutheran Church*, (Philadelphia: Board of Publication of the United Lutheran Church in America, 1918), 10.

3. *Ortho + praxy* = "correct practice" as opposed to *ortho + doxy* = "correct teaching."

4. As quoted in a daily devotional from the Center for Action and Contemplation, prepared by Fr. Richard Rohr.

5. See Psalm 24:1, NRSV: "The earth belongs to Yahweh, and all that is in it."

6. Walter Brueggemann, *Genesis* (Atlanta: John Knox Press, 1982).

7. Ibid., 27.

8. Mark 1:15; Peterson, *The Message*

9. John Dominic Crossan, *Jesus* (San Francisco: Harper One, 1994).

10. From a presentation made to Long Island clergy in Port Washington, New York, October 1999.

11. Powell, *Giving to God*, 87.

Chapter Nine

1. Coffin, *Credo*, 132.

2. As was noted in chapter 3, anxious people can become reactive, and reactive parishioners raise the stress level of pastors.

3. I later learned that this was a slight misquote. The actual quote is, "We cannot become what we want by remaining what we are" (Max De Pree, *Leadership Is an Art*).

4. Richard Hudnut-Beumler, *Generous Saints: Congregations Rethinking Ethics and Money* (Alban Institute, 1999), 5.

5. Lyle Schaller, *Strategies for Change* (Nashville, TN: Abingdon, 1993).

6. Ibid., 14.

7. D. Stephen Long is the Cary M. Maguire University professor of ethics at Southern Methodist University.

8. Milavec argues between 50–70 C.E.

9. Milavec, *The Didache*, 53.

10. Hall, *The Steward*, 9.

11. Smith and Emerson, *Passing the Plate*, 180.

12.   Diana Butler Bass, *Christianity after Religion: The End of Church and the Birth of a New Spiritual Awakening*, (Harper One, 2013), 37.

13.   Powell, *Giving to God*, p. 114.

14.   Ibid., 3.

15.   From a presentation that Fr. John made at a Ministry of Money event in October, 1991. See also "Chapter 5: Stewardly Discipleship" in Haughey, S.J., *Virtue and Affluence*.

16.   John Shea, Dinner conversation in Port Washington, NY, October 1998.

17.   William Sloan Coffin, from a sermon preached at the Riverside Church, New York, NY.

ABOUT THE AUTHOR

The Rev. Dr. Robert A. Hoffman, known to most as "Rip", developed an interest in American church history as an undergraduate. He continued to pursue that interest while in seminary. Rip did much of his doctoral study under the guidance of Robert Wood Lynn. They spent hours in Bob's living room in Portland, Maine, discussing the relationship between faith and money in American Protestantism. Rip served on the stewardship staff of his denomination. He has consulted with over 400 congregations across the denominations. When asked what he loves most about his work, his response is, "My greatest joy is seeing faith come alive."

CPSIA information can be obtained
at www.ICGtesting.com
Printed in the USA
BVHW081405150719
553470BV00005B/711/P